THE USSR AND SUB-SAHARAN AFRICA IN THE 1980s

DAVID E. ALBRIGHT

Foreword by Colin Legum

WITHDRAWN

Published with The Center for
Strategic and International Studies,
Georgetown University, Washington, D.C.

PRAEGER SPECIAL STUDIES • PRAEGER SCIENTIFIC

C 1

Library of Congress Cataloging in Publication Data

Albright, David E.
  The USSR and sub-Saharan Africa in the 1980's.

  (The Washington papers, ISSN 0278-937X; v. XI, 101)
  1. Africa, Sub-Saharan – Relations – Soviet Union.
  2. Soviet Union – Relations – Africa, Sub-Saharan.
  3. Africa, Sub-Saharan – Foreign relations – 1960–
  4. Africa, Sub-Saharan – Strategic aspects. I. Title.
  II. Title: U.S.S.R. and Sub-Saharan Africa in the
1980's. III. Series: Washington papers ; vol. XI, 101.
  DT353.5.S65A4   1983   327.67047   83–13699
  ISBN 0-03-069344-6

BURGESS
DT
353.5
.S65
A4
1983 *copy 1*

The *Washington Papers* are written under the auspices of The Center
for Strategic and International Studies (CSIS), Georgetown University,
and published with CSIS by Praeger Publishers. The views expressed in these
papers are those of the authors and not necessarily those of The Center.

Published in 1983 by Praeger Publishers
CBS Educational and Professional Publishing
a Division of CBS Inc.
521 Fifth Avenue, New York, New York 10175 U.S.A.

3456789 041 987654321

Printed in the United States of America

Contents

Foreword

In this impressive study David Albright rightly emphasizes the importance of the African factor, and not just that of Moscow's ambitions, in examining the opportunities and constraints on Soviet foreign policy in the continent. While I cannot agree in all respects with his interpretation of certain aspects of African policies or phenomena, my disagreements are not so great as to diminish my warm regard for his scholarship and his skills as a political analyst. His is an informed voice that deserves to be listened to with care and respect—especially at a time when U.S. foreign policy has entered upon another crucial stage of reexamining how to respond to the new challenges in the Third World.

A survey of Western and Marxist literature over the last three decades reveals how mistaken most students of Soviet policy have been in their analyses of the likely outcome of the USSR's involvement in Africa. Anti-Soviet writers (mainly Kremlinologists with little or no knowledge of Africa) tended to make two opposite errors. One group, especially in the 1950s and 1960s, envisaged a continent emerging from its colonial swaddling-clothes ready to fall into the embrace of the "anti-imperialist" forces of Marxism. Another group, especially in the late 1960s and up to 1974 (the year of the collapse of Portuguese colonialism), argued that neither the Soviet Union nor Marxism presented a serious threat to the West. After the dramatic Soviet and Cuban military intervention in Angola and Mozambique in the mid-1970s, much of the Western literature veered toward the position that a Soviet take-over was now a genuine threat and that periodic Western intervention would be required to block Moscow's advance right across the continent.

Soviet political analysts have been no more reliable than their Western counterparts. Their writings of the late 1950s sounded a high note of optimism — induced by such developments as Gamal Abd al-Nasser's alliance with Moscow, the decisions of President Sékou Touré of Guinea and President Kwame Nkrumah of Ghana to offer the USSR a role in West Africa, and by the opportunities opened up by the chaos in the Congo following Belgium's untidy termination of its colonial rule there in 1960. Subsequent events of the 1960s, however, taught Soviet policymakers and Soviet Africanists a great deal about the complexity of the African scene, with the result that even the apparent successes in Angola and Ethiopia have been treated with appropriate caution since the 1970s.

There has been one important exception to the generally faulty Soviet and Western forecasts made as the colonial era ended about the likely outcome of the Soviet Union's encounter with Africans. This was the accuracy with which a number of writers on African affairs (not, alas, Kremlinologists or Western specialists on military strategy) predicted that the Soviet bloc stood to make significant gains if Western policies (1) continued to favor the Salazar and Caetano regimes in their resistance to the growing popular pressure for independence in the Portuguese territories; (2) failed to take a more robust stand against the Unilateral Declaration of Independence (UDI) of the white Rhodesian regime headed by Ian Smith; and, (3) failed, over a longer term, to distance themselves from the apartheid regime in Pretoria. To my knowledge, however, no single political analyst predicted the Soviet *volte-face* in the Horn of Africa that gave Moscow the initiative in helping to guide the still uncompleted Ethiopian revolution.

It is, in fact, the policies pursued by most Western governments toward nationalist movements that account for Moscow's successes in Angola and Ethiopia, rather than any particular clever Soviet strategy or adventurous opportunism. In assessing the likely future role of the Soviet bloc in Africa, political analysts must focus as much on Western policies as on Moscow's. This is especially true with regard to the struggles now in being or taking shape in Southern Africa, where Western interests have traditionally been so closely identified with the South African economic system.

A remarkable phenomenon of Africa's post-colonial politics is the lack of appeal of Marxist ideology (particularly of the Moscow variety) to the continent's new political class. Marxist parties remain far weaker in Africa than in either Asia or Latin America and, of course, much weaker than in Western Europe. For a time it seemed that the Marxism of Mao would find fertile soil in an environment where the first generation of postindependence leaders had so conspicuously failed to deliver the fruits promised during the anticolonial struggle; although Maoism was initially widely felt to be more relevant to the needs and feelings of the Third World societies than the Soviet model, no influential Marxist movements of Maoist orientation have emerged.

It is interesting to reflect that the three strongest Communist parties on the continent—those in Egypt, Sudan, and South Africa—all developed in the preindependence period. The only significant Marxist parties to have developed since the ending of colonialism are the MPLA in Angola, Frelimo in Mozambique, and the putative Worker's Party of Ethiopia. Moreover, it is still much too early to make any large claims about the nature or durability of any of these parties. Frelimo, which grew up under Chinese rather than Soviet influence, is possibly the most developed of the new Communist parties in terms of meaningful political structures. The MPLA is, for the present, in a state of considerable disarray, with no effective popular structures. The Ethiopian Worker's Party is still in embryo.

Perhaps the most telling lesson that Soviet Marxists have learned from their African experience is that the USSR can win temporary successes in situations where a local power group needs a strategic ally to help it either to maintain or win power, but a more durable relationship depends on the development of effective vanguard Marxist parties, such as those in Eastern Europe. Only in the next phase in Africa's postcolonial history will we learn if conditions for the growth of such parties are now developing. This is the X-factor in any predictions one cares to venture about the likely future role of the Soviet Union on the continent.

Meanwhile, the operational mandate for African Communist parties would appear to be to pursue the well-tested tactic of promoting united fronts with progressive nationalist forces—especially with popular national liberation movements. But unless the Marxist cadres are sufficiently entrenched within these democratic fronts by the time power is acquired, they are liable to find themselves eliminated.

Soviet and Africanist policymakers have also learned that even Marxist-oriented regimes (such as those in Angola and Mozambique), are likely to turn anxiously to the West to ensure their survival when they discover that the Soviet Union and its allies are incapable of sustaining much trade or providing the needed level of economic aid and appropriate technical assistance. As David Albright points out, Moscow acknowledges the inability of the Comecon countries to fulfill these needs and therefore acquiesces in their protégé regimes opening their doors to Western interests; but this inevitably affects the client relationship with the fledgling Marxist states.

In summary, African regimes linked by choice or necessity to the Soviet Union are likely to behave no differently from those in, say, Yugoslavia, Czechoslovakia, Romania, or Poland. When national interests are seen to conflict with those of Moscow, they will resolutely seek to pursue an independent nationalist line. The important difference is that distant African countries are not so easily suborned when they choose to "deviate," as is the case with the regimes on the borders of the USSR.

Colin Legum
Editor of the *Africa Contemporary Record*

August 1983

Preface

This paper constitutes a revised and expanded version of a background study prepared for the project on factors affecting Soviet foreign policy in the 1980s sponsored by the Georgetown University Center for Strategic and International Studies during 1981–1982. I am indebted to Adam Ulam, chairman of the panel on external influences, and Robert Byrnes, director of the overall project, for asking me to address the issues discussed herein. Working with Adam Ulam proved especially congenial, for I found him not only willing but even eager to hear my views — on questions about which we ultimately disagreed as well as those on which we saw eye to eye. Aileen Masterson, coordinator for the project, also provided immeasurable aid on countless administrative matters connected with my participation in the undertaking.

I am particularly grateful to Helen Kitchen and Commander William Nurthen for reading drafts of the paper and giving me detailed suggestions for improving it. However, neither of them bears any responsibility for the contents of the final product. Nor do the judgments expressed in it necessarily reflect those of the U.S. Air Force or the U.S. government.

Last but by no means least, I want to thank my wife Ruth for her key contributions to the production of this paper. Not only did she type the final draft of the manuscript, but she also exercised great forbearance at the amount of my time that its preparation consumed. Indeed, her support and sacrifices were critical to the paper's emergence in printed form.

About the Author

David E. Albright is currently professor of national security affairs at the Air War College, Maxwell Air Force Base, Alabama. Previously, he worked for more than a decade at the journal *Problems of Communism*, serving first as associate editor and later as senior text editor. He has also been a research associate at the Council on Foreign Relations in New York City. Dr. Albright has written extensively on the Soviet Union and the Third World. Among his more recent publications on this topic are *Communism in Africa* (Indiana University Press, 1980); "The Middle East and Africa in Recent Soviet Policy," in Roger E. Kanet (ed.), *Soviet Foreign Policy in the 1980s* (Praeger, 1982); "The Communist States and Southern Africa," in Gwendolyn Carter and Patrick O'Meara (eds.), *The International Politics of Southern Africa* (Indiana University Press, 1982).

Introduction

The USSR today clearly is a major actor in sub-Saharan Africa. It has formal diplomatic relations with nearly every country of the region – the most important exceptions being Namibia and South Africa, both under white-minority rule. It even boasts formal treaties of friendship and cooperation with several states in the area. It furnishes substantial numbers of economic and military advisers to sub-Saharan African countries on a long- as well as short-term basis. It provides education or training to appreciable contingents of students and military personnel from the region. It extends some economic aid to sub-Saharan African states, and it engages in trade of not insignificant proportions with many countries of the area. It supplies the bulk of the weapons and equipment with which the remaining "national liberation" movements in the region carry on their militant struggles. It also ships large amounts of arms to sub-Saharan African governments. It even possesses capabilities to operate militarily in the area, whether on its own or in conjunction with surrogates.

Under such circumstances, it is appropriate to try to define precisely the present Soviet role in sub-Saharan Africa and to assess systematically the outlook for change in this role during the rest of the 1980s. These are the purposes of this paper.

The nature and depth of the USSR's involvement in sub-Saharan Africa in the 1980s reflects the onset of a new stage in Soviet-African relations in the 1970s. This new era, to be sure, does not represent a total departure from the past. On the contrary, Soviet activities with respect to the region assumed consequence as early as the late 1950s. But the differences between the Soviet role in the region prior to 1970 and that role during the 1970s – especially the last half of the 1970s – greatly outweighed the elements of continuity.

Therefore, Chapter 1 of this paper looks in detail at the shift that took place in the 1970s in the USSR's involvement in the region. It lays out the character and dimensions of the change and seeks to pinpoint the reasons for these. In addition, it endeavors to specify the limits of the new role that the USSR came to play in the area during these years.

Subsequent chapters explore factors that could conceivably alter Soviet involvement in the region in the next few years. Chapter 2 examines Moscow's objectives in sub-Saharan Africa and their bearing on the situation. Chapter 3 appraises existing and probable future opportunities for the USSR in the region, and Chapter 4 focuses on those opportunities most likely to attract Soviet attention. Chapter 5 deals with the constraints under which the USSR will in all probability have to operate in the area in the years ahead.

The final chapter then tries to assess the overall prospects with respect to the Soviet role in sub-Saharan Africa to the end of the 1980s. Here the emphasis is on identification of key factors that will determine the nature and scope of the involvement, rather than on straightforward prediction.

1

The Record of the 1970s

Significant Soviet involvement in sub-Saharan Africa began in 1958, after Guinea rejected association with France in favor of independence. Cast adrift politically and economically by France's irate President Charles de Gaulle, the fledgling African state searched desperately for an alternate patron, and Soviet Premier Nikita Khrushchev eagerly took on that role.

This initial relationship soon led to others. During the early 1960s, the regimes of Kwame Nkrumah in Ghana and Modibo Keita in Mali established close ties with the USSR. Indeed, after a temporary rift between Guinean President Ahmed Sékou Touré and Moscow in 1961, Ghana and Mali became the collective cornerstone of the Soviet position in the area. Well before the radical regimes of Nkrumah and Keita succumbed to military coups in the mid-1960s, however, the USSR had also expanded and diversified its contacts in the region. By the close of the decade, Moscow maintained official relations with 26 sub-Saharan African states of widely varying ideological orientation.

3

Soviet activities during this early period ranged across a broad spectrum. The great bulk of the $870 million in economic credits that the USSR offered to countries in the region between 1959 and 1974 was extended in the 1960s.[1] During the years before 1970, the USSR also delivered about $120 million in arms to the independent states of the area plus a small but undeterminable amount to "national liberation" movements there.[2] Along with the economic aid and supplies of arms went a variety of personnel. The number of Soviet economic technicians in sub-Saharan Africa had reached 300 by 1960, and by 1965 it had ballooned to 1,735. However, the figure then dropped somewhat, standing at 1,585 in 1970.[3] The contingent of military technicians grew more slowly but nevertheless steadily. By 1965, that of the USSR and Eastern Europe combined totaled 400, and by 1970 the number had risen to 965.[4] During the 1960s, Soviet educational institutions accepted substantial numbers of academic students from sub-Saharan Africa. By 1965, there were 4,985 students from the area in the USSR, and the figure had mounted to 6,260 by 1970.[5] Soviet trade with the region expanded appreciably as well. By 1965, the USSR's exports to sub-Saharan Africa had increased to $85 million, while its imports from there were running at $60 million. As of 1970, these sums had climbed to $95 million and $140 million respectively.[6]

Of equal importance, the USSR played at least a peripheral role in all the major crises that beset the region in the 1960s. The recurrent troubles in the Congo-Leopoldville (now Zaire) in the first half of the decade afford the outstanding example. During the initial months of the Congo's independence in 1960, Moscow forged links of some moment with the new state's premier, Patrice Lumumba, and when he requested Soviet help to restore the authority of his central government over the secessionist province of Katanga, the USSR responded with an offer of a sizable number of trucks and the planes to transport them from Leopoldville to Katanga. Lumumba's deposal by President Joseph Kasavubu and the Congolese military in the fall of 1960, however, brought a sharp turn in Soviet influence in the country. Although the USSR for a time supported a rump Lumumba regime based in Stanleyville, this regime eventually made peace with the central authorities in Leopoldville. As a result, Soviet involvement in the country declined drastically. That involvement increased briefly once again in 1964–1965, when the Congo suffered another wave of insurrection – particularly in its northern and eastern provinces. On this occasion, Moscow backed the disparate rebel forces led by, among others, Pierre Mulele, Christophe Gbenye, and Gaston-Emile Soumialot. The failure of the insurrectionists to topple the central government, however, produced another setback for the Soviets. Once more, Soviet involvement in Congolese affairs receded to a minimal level.

Not all Moscow's efforts in crisis situations netted the USSR as little as those in the Congo-Leopoldville ultimately did. Soviet undertakings during the Nigerian civil war of the late 1960s provide a good illustration. In reaction to an appeal by the central Nigerian government for substantial quantities of arms to meet the challenge posed by Biafra's attempted secession, Moscow shipped $29 million worth of weapons and equipment to Nigeria.[7] These arms contributed significantly to the central government's ability to reestablish its writ throughout the country. By furnishing them, Moscow earned Lagos's gratitude and set the stage for a more extensive relationship during the 1970s.

For all this involvement, however, the USSR did not by any means enjoy the prominence in sub-Saharan Africa during the 1960s that it attained during the ensuing decade. The new Soviet prominence manifested itself in both quantitative and qualitative terms.

The Quantitative Change

From a quantitative standpoint, Moscow made impressive strides in the political realm during the 1970s. It extended its web of official ties to virtually the whole region by establishing diplomatic relations with 14 additional countries.[8] This constituted, it should be noted, nearly a third of the area's 48 political entities (counting Zimbabwe, Namibia, South Africa, and the offshore island states).

More important, Soviet officials concluded treaties of friendship and cooperation with four sub-Saharan African countries—Somalia, Angola, Mozambique, and Ethiopia—although Somalia by the end of the 1970s had renounced the one which pertained to it.[9] Perhaps the most significant aspect of these documents was provision for consultation between the two signatories in the event of a security threat to either.[10] Prior to the 1970s, Moscow had maintained this kind of a treaty relationship only with Communist states.

On a more informal plane, the Communist Party of the Soviet Union (CPSU) forged links with four newly self-styled Marxist-Leninist ruling parties in the region—in Angola, Mozambique, Benin, and the People's Republic of the Congo—and one commission set up to create such a party—in Ethiopia. These ties encompassed advice on ideological and organizational work.[11]

Finally, the USSR emerged as the leading non-African patron of all those remaining national liberation movements of sub-Saharan Africa engaged in militant struggles, whether of a guerrilla or an urban terrorist sort. Until Moscow helped the Popular Movement for the Liberation of Angola (MPLA) take over control of the government in Angola during the civil war there in the mid-1970s, China had fulfilled that function for a majority of the movements.

Progress in the economic sphere was far more modest yet nonetheless of moment. Toward the end of the 1970s, Soviet

commitments of economic aid to sub-Saharan African countries picked up appreciably in comparison with those of the
immediately preceding years. During 1975-1979, states in
the region accepted pledges of $335 million of new credits
from Moscow, whereas the figure for the entire 1965-1974
decade had been only $380 million. The 1975-1979 total, how-
ever, fell short of the $490 million that the USSR had ten-
dered to countries in the area during 1959-1964.[12] This disparity, it should be stressed, apparently had much more
to do with Soviet perceptions of the utility of such assistance
for the USSR than from the reluctance of sub-Saharan Africans to receive this kind of help.

Indeed, the states of the region displayed no reserve
about expanding other forms of economic ties with the
USSR. The number of Soviet economic technicians in the
area, for example, nearly quadrupled over the decade. In
1970, it stood at 1,585. By 1975, it had reached 2,995, and
it hit 5,640 by 1979.[13] The contingent of students from sub-
Saharan African countries at Soviet educational institutions
doubled during the same time frame. In 1970, there were
6,260 students from the region in the USSR. The total had ris-
en to 8,040 by 1975, and by 1979 it had escalated to 12,865.[14]
Trade turnover between the states of sub-Saharan Africa and
the USSR also more than tripled during the 1970s. In 1970,
Soviet exports to the area amounted to $125 million, and its
imports, to $85 million. By the end of the decade, exports had
more than doubled, while imports had nearly quadrupled.[15]

The military domain saw the most spectacular Soviet advances. Sub-Saharan Africans in 1975-1979 accepted about
17 times the amount of weapons and equipment, in value
terms, than they had during the entire 1961-1971 decade.
Soviet arms deliveries to governments in the region in the
last half of the 1970s totaled $3,380 million, whereas the fig-
ure for 1961-1971 had reached just $182 million.[16] These
sums, to be sure, do not reflect the military aid that Moscow

provided to national liberation movements in the area during either period. Nevertheless, inclusion of this aid, the precise levels of which are unknown, would probably not alter the ratio much. Circumstantial evidence suggests that even though more movements existed during the 1961–1971 decade, they got less material support from Moscow than did the far smaller number still carrying on their struggles in the late 1970s.

The list of recipients of Soviet arms likewise lengthened somewhat. In 1961–1971, the number of states on the list was nine. It also encompassed six national liberation movements – in Angola, Cape Verde, Guinea-Bissau, Mozambique, Zimbabwe, and Namibia – that had not yet won independence by the 1970s and were waging guerrilla wars to that end. In 1975–1979, the total of recipients jumped to 19 sovereign countries plus national liberation movements in Zimbabwe and Namibia. But this figure included four states where weapons from the USSR had gone to local national liberation movements in the earlier years, so these states should not be counted as new recipients. At the same time, one country on the 1961–1971 roster – Ghana – dropped off in 1975–1979. Hence, there was a net increase of six recipients of Soviet arms in the 1975–1979 period.[17]

Far more critical, the region's dependence on Soviet arms shipments rose sharply. In 1961–1971, only four of the 14 states and national liberation movements that took arms from the USSR – Congo-Brazzaville, Guinea, Mali, and Somalia – relied on it as even their primary supplier. By 1975–1979, in contrast, four of the 21 entities that received weapons and equipment from the USSR – Cape Verde, Equatorial Guinea, Guinea, and Guinea-Bissau – obtained their arms exclusively from the Soviet Union, and 13 others – Angola, Benin, Chad, the Congo, Ethiopia, Madagascar, Mali, Mozambique, Nigeria, Tanzania, and Uganda, plus national liberation movements in Zimbabwe and Namibia – secured them primarily from Moscow.[18]

A significant expansion of various kinds of Soviet technical assistance accompanied the increase in the flow of arms. The contingent of Soviet and East European military technicians in sub-Saharan Africa grew from 965 in 1970 to 1,580 in 1975, and to 3,990 in 1979.[19] During 1978–1979, Soviet institutions provided training for 2,240 military personnel from sub-Saharan African countries. This figure compared with 8,600 for the entire 1959–1977 period.[20]

Of no less importance than the mounting dependence of the area on Moscow for arms and military advice and training was the growth of Soviet and Soviet-coordinated military forces in the area. The USSR in 1969 established a permanent naval presence in the Indian Ocean, off the east coast of sub-Saharan Africa, and this subsequently expanded to an average of 3 submarines, 7 surface combatants, and 18 support ships at any given instant.[21] In 1970, a small Soviet West Africa patrol began to operate in the eastern Atlantic near the western part of the region.[22] Then in the mid-1970s, Cuban combat troops came to sub-Saharan Africa. Although these were not mere extensions of Soviet forces, Havana tended to cooperate with Moscow on their employment.[23] As of the end of 1979, these troops, situated in Angola and Ethiopia, were estimated to number more than 30 thousand.[24]

The Qualitative Change

From a qualitative perspective, two things were salient. First, the USSR's relations with a few states and the national liberation movements in sub-Saharan Africa attained a degree of intimacy during the 1970s that exceeded anything evident in prior years. Some comparative details will help to illustrate the point.

The zenith in Soviet ties with independent governments of sub-Saharan Africa in the 1960s came in Ghana in the mid-1960s.[25] During the last years before Kwame Nkrumah's overthrow in February 1966, the Ghanaian president listened frequently to Soviet advice with respect to the conduct of Ghanaian affairs. For instance, Georgi Rodionov, Moscow's ambassador in Accra, had more ready access to and more powerful influence on Nkrumah than did many of Nkrumah's own ministers and officials. Moreover, the Ghanaian president had a Soviet economic adviser working closely with him on a full-time basis.

Nkrumah also relied heavily on Soviet assistance for his own personal protection during these years. For example, the USSR assumed responsibility for training and equipping his bodyguard. Even more important, Soviet personnel oversaw that bodyguard's expansion to serve as a counterweight to the regular armed forces. By February 1966, the Presidential Detail Department consisted of a 1st Guard Regiment composed of 50 officers and 1,142 men and a 2nd Guard Regiment undergoing formation and training. In addition, Soviet intelligence specialists became involved in several types of activity connected with the uncovering and suppression of domestic dissent in Ghana.

Although Nkrumah had by this juncture reduced Ghana's one legal party, the Convention People's Party, to little more than a hollow shell, he looked to Moscow for help to transform it into a personal ideological instrument. About half of the 28 regular members of the 1965–1966 faculty of the Kwame Nkrumah Institute of Economics and Political Science were from the USSR and Eastern Europe or belonged to Communist Parties in the West.

The Ghanaians sought aid from the USSR in other significant spheres too. By the mid-1960s, a number of Russians were teaching at the University of Ghana, and one of those in the Faculty of Law was drawing up proposals for Nkrumah concerning the restructuring of the university. Furthermore, by the latter part of 1965, Soviet doctors constituted virtually the entire staff of Ghana's lone medical college, and Soviet educators made up one-third of all the qualified instructors of math and science in the country's secondary schools.

Nkrumah showed his gratitude to Moscow in various ways during this period. He reacted favorably to Soviet solicitations for his support on international matters of both major and minor import to the USSR. For instance, he embarked on a vitriolic campaign against NATO's proposed multilateral force in 1965 in response to Moscow's request for backing of its drive to induce the West to bury the already foundering scheme permanently. He sanctioned growing Ghanaian participation in the myriad united front organizations that the USSR dominated. He even allowed Soviet personnel to construct on Ghanaian soil facilities of particular benefit to the USSR. Among these were a monitoring station and a large military airfield capable of handling jet aircraft. The Soviets seemingly conceived the latter as a staging point between the USSR and Cuba.

This apparent closeness of Soviet-Ghanaian relations, however, tended to obscure some critical realities. To begin with, the USSR's political status in Ghana rested upon rather fragile foundations. Despite the "socialist" rhetoric that pervaded the state's public discourse in the 1960s, very few Ghanaians held genuinely Marxist views; hence, there was not much ideological affinity for the USSR in the country. Nor did the Soviet physical presence in the state ever number more than about 1,000 people, counting dependents as well as working personnel. Moreover, the Soviet entanglement with Nkrumah personally linked Soviet fortunes to an individual, and during the last years of the Ghanaian president's rule, Nkrumah became increasingly isolated politically as he behaved more and more despotically and as his personality cult grew.

Circumstances in other spheres did nothing to offset these factors. The less than $100 million in economic credits that Moscow extended to the Nkrumah government in 1960 and 1961 represented a mere drop in the bucket compared with Western investments in and Western aid to Ghana. To make matters worse, Accra as late as the end of 1964 had exhausted less than 27 percent of the total credits that the USSR had offered. Furthermore, Ghana's trade turnover with the Soviet Union barely exceeded 5 percent of Ghana's total foreign commerce in any year, and its exports invariably surpassed its imports.[26] During the 1960s, Ghana did take about $10 million in arms from the USSR, but the Ghanaian armed forces still remained largely dependent on the West for their weapons and equipment.[27] Perhaps of greater significance, the USSR did not succeed in gaining the sort of foothold in the structure of the armed forces that they enjoyed in the intelligence apparatus. Indeed, they lacked even a toehold there.

All these realities sprang to the fore in 1966 with Nkrumah's ouster. Practically overnight the great bulk of the links that had existed between the USSR and Ghana vanished.

The most extensive ties that the USSR developed in sub-Saharan Africa in the 1970s were with Angola, Ethiopia, and Mozambique. In certain respects these resembled Soviet-Ghanaian relations of the mid-1960s.

For example, the leaders of all three states displayed considerable willingness to accept Soviet advice and help in handling their countries' domestic affairs. In Angola, the MPLA relied in part on Soviet military advisers in conducting the last stages of the civil war of 1975–1976, and after it succeeded in establishing itself as the legal ruler of Angola, it continued to draw upon their services. It employed them to build up military forces to cope with the persisting insurgency in the south by Jonas Savimbi and his National Union for the Total Independence of Angola (UNITA), as well as with South African attacks against guerrillas of the Southwest Africa People's Organization (SWAPO) of Namibia and their base camps on Angolan territory.[28] Similarly, Ethiopia's Provisional Military Administrative Council (Derg) enlisted a team of Soviet advisers headed by the first deputy commander of Soviet ground forces to direct its 1977–1978 drive to throw Somalia's military forces out of the Ogaden. Although the highest ranking members of this team quickly returned to the USSR in the wake of Somalia's defeat in early 1978, the Derg still kept a contingent of Soviet officers on the scene to aid it in dealing with the rebellion of Eritrea.[29] The governing elements of all three states also consulted with Soviet specialists about local ideological work. This consultation took diverse forms. All three countries, for instance, dispatched delegations on tours to examine ideological operations in the USSR. Angola and Mozambique even apparently invited cadres from the CPSU and pro-Soviet East European Communist Parties to lend a hand with local ideological activities, but information on the precise number of such cadres is unavailable.[30] Although none of the three states involved the USSR directly in shaping or reshaping their intelligence and security services, they did call upon its closest East European ally, the German Democratic Republic (GDR), for assistance in this regard. GDR advisers supplied the instruction for these services and reportedly even trained the personal bodyguards of Samora Machel, president of Mozambique, and Mengistu Haile-Mariam, chairman of Ethiopia's Derg.[31]

In addition, the three countries evinced solidarity with the USSR in ways especially gratifying to Moscow. For instance, all gave strong backing to Soviet positions on many international issues. Perhaps the most dramatic illustration came just as the 1970s ended and a new decade began. The three voted against the UN resolution demanding the withdrawal of the Soviet troops that had invaded Afghanistan in December 1979. Aside from the USSR's fellow members of the Council of Mutual Economic Assistance (CMEA), the only other states to do so were Afghanistan itself, Grenada, and South Yemen. Angola and Ethiopia also accorded the USSR access to some facilities useful for military purposes. The Angolan government allowed ships of the Soviet West Africa patrol to call at the port of Luanda and Soviet planes to use the Luanda airport for reconnaissance flights over the Atlantic sea lanes, while the Ethiopian government permitted the USSR to establish an upkeep operation in one of the Dahlak Islands off Massawa for Soviet ships in the Indian Ocean-Red Sea area and to send reconnaissance aircraft into and out of the Johannes IV airport.[32]

Finally, the economic relations of the three states with the USSR did not amount to much. During the entire 1970s, Moscow extended a paltry $5 million in economic credits to Mozambique, and the figure for Angola was not much higher — $15 million. The USSR did offer Ethiopia $125 million in economic aid over the decade, but that figure failed to match Western economic assistance. Even if the comparison is confined to the last half of the 1970s, when radicalization of Ethiopian politics produced a decline in Western credits, there was still an imbalance in favor of the West.[33] Contradictory statistics make it impossible to determine just how important trade with the USSR became in the overall trade of these countries, but the available evidence suggests that none of the three had a trade turnover with the USSR that came close to 10 percent of its total trade turnover, although the Soviet share of Angola's imports in at least one year in the late 1970s may have run about that high.[34]

Yet Soviet involvement with Angola, Mozambique, and Ethiopia in the 1970s differed significantly from Soviet involvement with Ghana in the mid-1960s. To begin with, there was far greater depth to the political ties in the case of the three. As a result of the rigors of the liberation struggle, both the MPLA and the Front for the Liberation of Mozambique (FRELIMO) had undergone a radicalization process prior to their accession to power in the mid-1970s; thus, their ranks contained a fair number of dedicated Marxists. The situation was less striking in Ethiopia but nonetheless clear. Although the Derg ultimately turned savagely upon the civilian Marxists with whom it cooperated for a time, the radicalization of the military government that took place during the course of the Ethiopian revolution of the mid-1970s did bring to prominence several committed ideologues. This internal makeup of the ruling circles of the three states afforded a higher degree of commonality of viewpoint with the USSR than had existed in the earlier Ghanaian instance.[35]

The greater commonality of viewpoint, in turn, laid the groundwork for forms of mutual political cooperation that held promise of at least reducing any adverse effects for Moscow of changes of leadership in the three countries. For example, the ruling elements of Angola and Mozambique sought counsel from the CPSU and pro-Soviet East European Communist Parties about not just ideological undertakings but also organization work.[36] Such requests for inputs reflected their concerted efforts to form vanguard parties in their countries. (In contrast, Mengistu dragged his feet with respect to creating such a party in Ethiopia.[37]) No less important, the governments of all three countries entered into 20-year treaties of friendship and cooperation with the USSR.

Although, as previously noted, Soviet economic links with the three states remained weak, these were not totally devoid of elements of strength that had not been present in the prior Ghanaian situation. In the case of Ethiopia, the signing of a framework agreement for economic cooperation in 1978 substantially improved the chances for a long-term growth of economic ties. Among the more momentous steps later taken under the umbrella of this agreement was Soviet supply of oil to Ethiopia at preferential prices.[38] Addis Ababa's acceptance of such an arrangement rendered it markedly dependent on Moscow for this crucial import. Perhaps more salient, all three countries drew heavily upon the USSR for technical assistance. By 1979, the total number of Soviet and East European economic technicians in Angola had reached 2,760. The figure for Mozambique was 800; that for Ethiopia, 1,500.[39]

It was in the military domain, however, that the contrasts manifested themselves most profoundly. Whereas the USSR had served as a decidedly secondary source of arms for Ghana in the 1960s, it emerged as the primary source for Angola, Mozambique, and Ethiopia during the 1970s. Indeed, its deliveries of weapons and equipment to the three greatly surpassed those of any other single supplier. Soviet arms transfers to Angola in 1975–1979 accounted for $500 million of the $890 million that Luanda received during those years; those to Mozambique, $170 million of the $240 million that Maputo got; those to Ethiopia, $1,500 million of the $1,800 million that Addis Ababa received.[40]

There were other major connections as well between the armed forces of the three states and the USSR. In the wake of the Angolan civil war, 1,000 Soviet officers assumed positions on at least a temporary basis in the Angolan military and command structure. By 1979, the number of Soviet and East European military technicians in Mozambique had risen to 525. That same year, the figure for Ethiopia hit 1,250.[41] All three countries, moreover, sent not inconsequential numbers of military personnel to the USSR for training. In 1977–1979, 55 Angolans, 400 Mozambicans, and 1,290 Ethiopians went through training programs there.[42] Last but by no means least, both the Angolan and Ethiopian governments sanctioned the stationing of large numbers of troops from

Cuba, one of the USSR's close allies, on their national soil. As of the end of 1979, there were an estimated 19 thousand Cuban combat soldiers in Angola and 13 thousand in Ethiopia.[43]

With respect to the national liberation movements of sub-Saharan Africa, none during the 1960s treated the USSR as anything more than one of several key supporters. Many of the movements in the area did solicit and obtain Soviet endorsement during these years, and a number of those engaged in guerrilla struggles even secured some military aid from Moscow. The MPLA of Angola, for instance, forged links with the USSR in the early part of the decade and received assistance from it more or less continuously thereafter. Later, FRELIMO, SWAPO of Namibia, and the Zimbabwe African People's Union (ZAPU) did the same. Yet the USSR was never of vital importance in the perspectives of most members of these movements.[44]

During the 1970s, however, the great bulk of those naional liberation movements that had not yet won power—essentially the ones in Southern Africa—came to accord the USSR the status of crucial backer. The Angolan civil war and its outcome provided the catalyst here. For some time previously, the movements in question had forecast that they would have to pursue their objectives by violent means. Later they had concluded that they had no hope of even approaching the fulfillment of their goals without demonstrating real prowess on the battlefield. The Angolan affair convinced the vast majority of the participants in these movements that the USSR was the only force—African or otherwise—capable of effectively helping them to meet this requirement and potentially disposed to do so. Therefore, the USSR took on a new dimension in their eyes, and they proceeded to strengthen their ties with Moscow.[45] During subsequent years, for instance, the USSR became the chief source of arms for ZAPU and SWAPO, although in the case of ZAPU Moscow turned this function over to the GDR, its main East European ally, before the end of the decade.[46]

The second major qualitative sign during the 1970s of the increased importance of the USSR in sub-Saharan Africa concerned Moscow's role in crises in the region. As mentioned previously, the USSR had participated in one way or another in all the area's key crises during the 1960s, yet it had not been a central actor in any of them. That situation altered during the succeeding decade.

Angola's civil war of 1975–1976 constituted the watershed in this regard. After attempts to form a coalition government embracing the MPLA and two rival national liberation groups, UNITA and the National Front for the Liberation of Angola (FNLA), broke down in the summer of 1975, the Soviet Union collaborated with Cuba and the GDR to install the MPLA in power.

The USSR's contributions to the effort lay largely in the realm of logistics, but these contributions were absolutely vital to the ultimate success of the undertaking. In late 1975 and early 1976, Soviet planes airlifted Cuban combat forces and Soviet and East German advisers to Angola to assist the MPLA against the newly formed FNLA-UNITA coalition and invading military units from South Africa. At its peak in March 1976, the Cuban contingent alone consisted of 36 thousand combat troops. Not only did Moscow commit many aircraft to the transfer of troops and advisers to the scene, but it also transported large quantities of weapons and military equipment – worth about $400 million – by air and sea to Angola. The arms included surface-to-surface missiles, the hand-held SMA-7 antiaircraft missile, 122 mm katyusha rockets, T-34 and T-54 tanks, PT-76 amphibious tanks, armored reconnaissance vehicles (BRDM-2), trucks, helicopters, gunships, heavy artillery, light aircraft, and even MiG-21 planes. To protect the supply operation, the USSR maintained a naval squadron off shore, with access to facilities at Conakry, Guinea.[47]

For the first time, then, the USSR emerged as a critical player in the evolution and outcome of a significant regional crisis. Soon thereafter, it repeated that performance in the conflict between Ethiopia and Somalia over the Ogaden.[48] Moscow had long had links with Somalia, which claimed the Ogaden, a region under Ethiopian rule but populated predominantly by Somali-speaking peoples. Indeed, the USSR had even acquired access to the port of Berbera for various military purposes and to a number of Somali airfields to carry out reconnaissance flights over the Indian Ocean-Red Sea area. But in the mid-1970s, Soviet leaders opted to court the more and more revolutionary Derg of Ethiopia. To facilitate this undertaking, they sought to serve as peacemaker in the Horn of Africa by promoting a federal scheme to deal with the Ogaden problem. They envisioned the creation of (1) a federation of a Marxist Ethiopia embracing the Ogaden and (2) a larger federation of Marxist states encompassing Ethiopia, Somalia, the People's Democratic Republic of Yemen, and even Djibouti. This scheme, however, met resistance from both Somalia and Ethiopia.

The USSR finally adopted a different approach in the fall of 1977. In July 1977, President Mohamed Siad Barre of Somalia had sought to confront Moscow with a fait accompli by sending the Somali army into the Ogaden, but this force had bogged down before it seized all the disputed territory. Siad Barre had then, in mid-November, tried to win Western political and military support for his venture by kicking the Soviets out of his country and tearing up the Soviet-Somali treaty of friendship and cooperation. Moscow responded by throwing its weight heavily behind Ethiopia.

In collaboration with Cuba and to a lesser extent the GDR, the USSR undertook a massive military buildup in Ethiopia. A huge airlift of weapons and military equipment began toward the end of November. Such a sense of urgency pervaded the effort that Soviet planes filed misleading flight plans at refueling stations and flew over some states without permission in order to reach Ethiopia as quickly as possible. A big influx of Cuban and Soviet personnel accompanied the large infusions of arms. By early March 1978, Moscow had poured about $1 billion of weapons and equipment into the African country, and U.S. intelligence sources estimated that 11,000 Cuban and 1,000 Soviet advisers had arrived there, with more Cubans on the way by ship.

In early February 1978, the Ethiopians launched a major offensive under the guidance of General Vasilii Ivanovich Petrov, deputy commander of all Soviet ground forces, and with Cuban troops led by General Arnaldo Ochoa, Cuba's deputy minister of defense, spearheading the drive. This offensive rapidly overwhelmed the Somalis. By early March, the Somali army, after a disastrous defeat at Jijiga was no longer an effective military force, and Siad Barre announced that he was withdrawing all regular Somali units from the Ogaden.

This denouement, it is true, did not amount to a final solution of the problem, for Siad Barre vowed that the struggle for the "liberation" of the Ogaden would continue. Nevertheless, it did end the immediate hostilities that had caused the Somali-Ethiopian conflict to escalate to a crisis. And the USSR clearly had determined the precise resolution of that crisis.

Why the Change?

Several factors contributed to this enlargement of the Soviet role in sub-Saharan Africa during the 1970s. Although these were intertwined to some degree, each had its own distinctive impact.

The first was the continuing process of decolonization. During the mid-1970s, the military coup in Lisbon brought about the collapse of the Portuguese empire and catapulted all the Portuguese colonies in sub-Saharan Africa to independence. There were five of them—Angola, Cape Verde, Guinea-Bissau, Mozambique, and São Tomé and Principe. In addition, four other territories had attained, or virtually attained, sovereignty by the close of the decade. This group included Comoros, Djibouti, Seychelles, and Zimbabwe. Such a process improved the Soviet position in the area in fairly simple ways. It expanded the pool of entities with which the USSR could have formal dealings, and it swelled the ranks of possible collaborators with the USSR in "anti-imperialist" activities.

Another influence at work was a radicalization of the region. This did not take place uniformly across sub-Saharan Africa. Indeed, it was far more pronounced in some countries than in others. Nor did it proceed at a steady pace. At times, reversals occurred in specific places; on other occasions, there were dramatic leaps forward in certain states. Nor did the process flow from the same causes everywhere. In some instances, it grew out of turnovers of governments or rulers; in others, it resulted from shifts in the outlooks of leaders. Even the mode of change of government or rulers differed from one case to another. Sometimes, the transition came about by force, often with a degree of violence; sometimes, it was the outgrowth of the death, retirement, or—much more rarely—the electoral defeat of a leader. Nonetheless, the general trend was unmistakable.

Perhaps it evinced itself most visibly in the growing number of governments in sub-Saharan Africa that styled themselves Marxist-Leninist. In late 1969, that of the People's Republic of the Congo became the first to do so. During the course of the 1970s, eight others followed suit. The list included those of Benin, Somalia, Angola, Mozambique, Guinea-Bissau, São Tomé and Principe, Ethiopia, and Madagascar.

The drift manifested itself in a negative sense as well. "African socialism"—depicted as a specifically African type of development, different from Western capitalism and Eastern socialism – suffered a drastic loss of adherents during the 1970s. In fact, this African humanistic approach to socialism, much in vogue during the 1960s, had few defenders by the end of the decade. Even Julius Nyerere of Tanzania, a staunch proponent of the idea of a third, African path of development, now felt compelled to stress that the only difference between the "African" socialism of Tanzania and the "Marxist" socialism of Mozambique was one of "rhetoric."[49]

By and large, radicalization of the political environment in sub-Saharan Africa enhanced the USSR's chances of evolving intimate relations with many ruling or opposition elements within the region. Greater similarity of perspectives, after all, made it easier to find mutually acceptable grounds for cooperation.

Yet this radicalization, it should be underscored, by no means assured such intimacy. For example, while Somalia maintained strong ties with Moscow throughout the opening half of the 1970s, it had a falling out with the USSR in 1977 not long after Siad Barre proclaimed it a Marxist-Leninist state. Furthermore, Madagascar's verbal embrace of Marxism-Leninism did not result in the establishment of a particularly close relationship with the USSR.

A final factor that helped to enhance Soviet prominence in the area during the 1970s was a widespread transformation in sub-Saharan African attitudes toward the USSR. This transformation had several dimensions.[50]

First, leeriness of Moscow faded significantly. Prior to independence, few persons in the region had had any direct contacts with the USSR, and a high percentage of those who had – for example, George Padmore, who strongly influenced the development of Kwame Nkrumah's views on Pan-Africanism – had turned sharply against Moscow as a consequence of their experiences. They contended that Soviet authorities merely wanted to exploit African concerns for Soviet purposes. The USSR's behavior in the early 1960s reinforced this negative image for many in the area. Moscow supported a number of Marxist and other groups that challenged the initial independent governments (for example, in Cameroon and Kenya), and it intervened in power struggles going on within some postindependence governments (for example, Congo-Leopoldville and Guinea). Furthermore, Soviet officials tended to handle leaders of sub-Saharan African countries in a ham-handed fashion. Perhaps the most glaring illustration was their constant badgering of African leaders to identify with the USSR against the West and China. But by the early 1970s, a large majority of attentive sub-Saharan Africans had come to look upon the USSR as just another great power engaged in a worldwide competition for influence, power, and trade. Moreover, even though they suffered no illusions that Soviet authorities acted from selfless motives, they evinced a natural emotional response to the anti-imperialist packaging in which Moscow wrapped Soviet undertakings.

Second, there was a growing conviction that ties with the USSR could carry positive benefits. During the early and mid-1960s, the great bulk of the leaders of sub-Saharan Africa had feared that extensive dealings with Moscow would compromise their commitment to nonalignment. By the 1970s, however, a large proportion of the leaders in the region had concluded that links with the USSR could afford them more leverage over Soviet policies than they might otherwise enjoy. In addition, they believed that accepting economic aid from the USSR and engaging in trade with it not only posed no threats to their nonalignment but could even be advantageous to them.

Third, many sub-Saharan Africans now perceived that they could use the Soviet Union in various ways to further their own ends. During the 1960s, a few governments and opposition groups in the region, unable to obtain backing from the West to sustain themselves, had viewed the USSR in such a fashion and had turned to Moscow for help. Good illustrations of this sense of a temporary convergence of interests with the USSR were Guinea in the early days of its independence and the national liberation movements of Portuguese Africa. But during the 1970s the number of governments and opposition groups that saw the Soviet Union in a similar light rose dramatically. This was especially true after Moscow's intervention in the Angolan civil war.

Such a transformation in attitudes had profound implications for Soviet activities in the region. It rendered sub-Saharan Africans not just receptive but even eager for expansion of relations with the USSR.

Limits of the Soviet Role

To round out the picture of the escalation of Soviet involvement in sub-Saharan Africa during the 1970s, it is essential to spell out the limits of the USSR's new role in the region. Although the USSR took on increased importance in the area, it by no means acquired the status of hegemon there. For convenience of discussion, it is useful to talk about these limits in terms of the political, economic, and military aspects of the Soviet role.

Political Limits

As for the political aspect, Moscow could not mobilize the countries of sub-Saharan Africa at will in support of the Soviet position on international issues of import to the USSR. The states of the region adopted stances consistent with their own judgments of the merits of issues and with their own perceived interests. Whenever they happened to find these compatible with the Soviet posture, they had no problem lending their backing to Moscow. By the same token, however, they did not hesitate to oppose the USSR if they felt the situation demanded such a course. Perhaps the classic illustration concerned the Afghanistan imbroglio. Only three sub-Saharan African countries voted with the USSR against the UN resolution calling upon Moscow to withdraw its troops from Afghanistan.

Nor could Moscow gratuitously interfere in the domestic affairs of states in the region without great risk to Soviet interests. Especially in countries whose leaders felt little ideological affinity with the USSR, such behavior often produced sharp reactions. At one juncture during the decade, for example, Idi Amin of Uganda expelled Moscow's ambassador in Kampala in retaliation for, among other things, the USSR's withholding of spare parts for Soviet-supplied equipment of the Ugandan army and Soviet insistence that Ugandan pilots obtain the approval of Soviet officials before receiving permission to fly. Although Amin expressed gratitude for the military aid that the USSR had furnished, he lectured Moscow not to try to dictate to him what to do for the people of Uganda.[51] Even the more radical states of the area saw fit at times to upbraid the USSR for local activities that they deemed out of bounds. For instance, Angola's Agostino Neto, after putting down an attempted coup of which he believed Soviet officials had had prior knowledge, spoke publicly about the need to defend "the independence of the party [MPLA]" from outside interference.[52] Similarly, Ethiopia's Mengistu took umbrage at Soviet and Cuban pressure to set up a vanguard party.[53]

In addition, the USSR had no magic formula for preventing an erosion of its position in individual countries of sub-Saharan Africa. Indeed, it experienced severe setbacks in a number of places in the area during the 1970s. The ousters of Francisco Macias Nguema of Equatorial Guinea and Idi Amin of Uganda in 1979, for example, wiped out most of the ties that Moscow had built up with these states over the course of the decade. Widespread popular revulsion at the tyrannical rule of the two despots tarnished the image of all associated with them, and because the USSR had supplied arms to both, it suffered accordingly. Elsewhere, events of a different nature produced similar consequences. In the early 1970s, President Ja'far Numeri of the Sudan turned against his erstwhile Soviet allies in the wake of an attempted coup by the originally highly supportive local communists, for he believed that the plotters had at least had contact with Soviet embassy personnel.[54] A few years later, President Siad Barre of Somalia showed his displeasure with Soviet courtship of Ethiopia by tearing up the treaty of friendship and cooperation that he had signed with the USSR, expelling Soviet military advisers from his country, and denying the Soviets further use of Somali sea and air facilities.

Finally, Moscow did not become the dominant factor in the outcomes of all regional crises. Whatever the degree of Soviet encouragement of the former Katangese gendarmes who invaded Zaire's Shaba Province from bases in Angola in the spring of 1978, the USSR did not determine the results of this undertaking. It was France and Belgium, with the aid of the United States, that provided the decisive inputs by mounting a military counteroffensive on behalf of the Mobutu government. Nor did Moscow prove any more effective in shaping the resolution of the internal conflict between whites and blacks in Zimbabwe (Rhodesia) – despite strong Soviet backing for the black-controlled Patriotic Front and particularly its ZAPU wing under Joshua Nkomo. Great Britain, with the active cooperation of the United States, brought the contending parties to the conference table at Lancaster House in London in 1979 and induced them to work out an accord. Moreover, the Zimbabwe African National Union (ZANU), headed by Robert Mugabe, succeeded in relegating the Soviet-favored ZAPU to a highly secondary role by winning a parliamentary majority in the elections that followed in early 1980.

Economic Limits

With respect to the economic dimension of the Soviet role, Moscow possessed virtually no means to exert leverage in sub-Saharan Africa. This was true not only for the region as a whole but for individual countries as well.

The $335 million in credits that the USSR extended to states in the area in 1975–1979 – the part of the decade during which Moscow offered the bulk of its commitments, in value terms – represented but a minute share of the financial resources made available to the region during these years. For instance, actual financial flows to sub-Saharan Africa from the Western industrial countries, the member states of the Organization of Petroleum Exporting Countries (OPEC), and multilateral agencies amounted to nearly $57 billion during the period. This figure included private investments as well as technical cooperation, government aid, loans, and voluntary assistance. If one restricts the total to concessional flows – i.e., funds designated specifically for economic development and involving a grant element of at least 25 percent of the sum – it still reached about $35 billion.[55]

A similar situation prevailed in the cases of the particular recipients of Soviet economic aid. Ethiopia and Somalia were the biggest beneficiaries of Soviet largesse in 1975–1979, obtaining $125 million and $45 million respectively in commitments from Moscow. Actual financial flows from the Western industrial countries, the member states of OPEC, and multilateral agencies ran to about $725 million for Ethiopia and about $1,130 million for Somalia. Concessional flows alone were roughly $700 million and $920 million for the two respectively.[56] It should be pointed out, however, that by early 1980 the USSR had agreed to procure petroleum for Ethiopia at reduced prices. Because Ethiopia produced no petroleum itself and by 1979 was expending more than 40 percent of its export earnings on petroleum, this commitment did give Moscow a measure of potential influence that it had not enjoyed previously.[57]

It would appear that the contingent of 5,640 Soviet economic technicians in sub-Saharan Africa by the close of the 1970s fell well shy of the combined total of economic technicians there under the auspices of non-Communist governments, multilateral agencies, and private Western organizations. In fact, the same seems to have been the case even if one lumps together with Soviet economic specialists the 13,185 economic specialists that the USSR's East European and Cuban allies had in the area. Although aggregate figures on non-Communist economic technicians present in the region in the late 1970s are not available, the data at hand do suffice to uphold the preceding judgments. For example, there were at least twice as many British and French personnel in the area as there had been during the colonial era 20 or more years previously.[58]

Concentration of Soviet and Soviet bloc technical assistance on a relatively few countries, to be sure, rendered it of greater significance to these countries than to others. In 1979, Angola accounted for 2,760 of the Soviet and East European economic technicians in sub-Saharan Africa; Ethiopia, for 1,500; Guinea, for 645; Mali, for 485; Mozambique, for 800; and Nigeria, for 1,725. Of these states, Angola also had 6,500 Cuban economic technicians; Ethiopia, 450; Guinea, 200; and Mozambique, 600.[59] Yet at no time did any of these countries rely exclusively on technical aid from the USSR and its allies. Indeed, only in Angola during the initial years of its independence did the level of Soviet bloc technical assistance appear to be genuinely competitive with the level of that from other sources, and the MPLA government had begun to alter this circumstance considerably before the end of the decade. It was striking a large number of bilateral deals with individual Western firms willing to establish joint companies and invest in Angola's economic development.[60]

In the sphere of trade, the USSR was an exceedingly minor partner for sub-Saharan Africa during the entire decade. Even if one excluded South Africa, with which the Soviet Union had no direct commercial contacts (although there were persistent reports of indirect economic linkages), Moscow took only about 1 percent of the region's exports in any year from 1975 through 1979, and it provided no more than 1 percent, and sometimes even less, of its imports in any year of the same period. By way of comparison, the Western industrial states in 1975–1979 accounted for an average of 73 percent of the world sales to black African countries and an average of 75 percent of their purchases from the world each of these years.[61]

For individual states, it is true, the USSR did look more important as a trading partner, but the difference tended to be marginal in character. During 1975–1979, for example, Moscow rarely supplied as much as 10 percent of the imports or bought as much as 10 percent of the exports of those countries in the region with which it had the largest commercial dealings. Its performance hit this level most often in the cases of Guinea and Ghana. The USSR evidently was the source of 10–15 percent of Guinea's purchases from abroad in 1975, 1976, and 1977, and it took 10–15 percent of Conakry's exports in 1975 and 1976. Soviet imports from Ghana ran to 10–15 percent of the African state's total sales abroad every year from 1976 through 1979. In other instances, Moscow managed to reach such a level only sporadically. The USSR accounted for 10–15 percent of Somalia's imports in both 1975 and 1976. In 1975, Moscow bought about 10 percent of Cameroon's exports, and about 15 percent of Guinea-Bissau's imports that same year came from the USSR. To put these figures in perspective, it is useful to bear in mind that the Western industrial states never failed to furnish more than half of the imports or to absorb more than half of the exports of any one of these countries throughout the 1975–1979 period.[62]

Military Limits

In regard to the military side of the Soviet role, it was clear that the majority of the states of sub-Saharan Africa still remained leery of ties with the USSR in this realm. During 1975–1979, for instance, only 38 governments in the region felt the need to obtain arms from external sources, and fully half of these did not acquire any Soviet weapons and equipment. In contrast, all but 11 accepted arms from the United States and its NATO allies.[63]

Most of the states that received Soviet arms, moreover, recognized a utility in getting weapons and equipment from diverse sources. Just 4 of the 19 governments that took Soviet arms in 1975–1979 relied solely on the USSR for deliveries of weapons and equipment. Of the 15 others, 12 even procured arms from the United States and its NATO allies. As a matter of fact, 8 of the latter governments were among the 11 for which Moscow served as primary supplier of weapons and equipment.[64]

Even in cases where states and national liberation movements became heavily dependent on arms from the USSR because of the scope of their perceived needs and/or difficulty in acquiring weapons and equipment from alternative sources, these entities typically sought to preserve their freedom of action in all spheres, so military dependence on the Soviet Union did not inevitably give Moscow influence with them. Indeed, Soviet efforts to pressure the recipients to adopt policies not to their liking frequently created major problems for the USSR. For example, as the Angolan situation heated up during 1975, Moscow tried to induce Idi Amin of Uganda, the current chairman of the Organization of African Unity (OAU), to side with the MPLA, but Soviet arm-twisting managed only to anger Amin. His ire at this and other aspects of Soviet behavior prompted him, in turn, to send the Soviet ambassador in Kampala packing.[65] Somalia in 1977 afforded a far more dramatic illustration. In the early part of the year, Soviet authorities, eager to expand their relations with Ethiopia, attempted to bring about a reconciliation between the feuding governments in Mogadishu and Addis Ababa by promoting the formation of a Red Sea Marxist federation incorporating both countries. President Siad Barre of Somalia not only rejected this plan but in July dispatched regular Somali forces into the disputed Ogaden in defiance of Soviet wishes. More telling yet, after Moscow elected to serve as peacemaker and moved to cut off Somalia's flow of arms to further this end, Siad Barre severed Somalia's military ties with the USSR.[66]

Although Angola and Ethiopia constituted special cases in light of their acceptance of substantial numbers of Cuban combat troops in addition to large quantities of Soviet arms, they too showed a determination not to be mere pawns of Moscow. The Mengistu government in Ethiopia, for instance, persisted in seeking to subdue the rebellious Eritreans by force despite clear Soviet and Cuban preference for a negotiated solution to conflict.[67] It also failed to yield to Soviet urgings to form a true vanguard party. The MPLA government in Angola, for its part, cooperated with undertakings aimed at resolving civil conflicts between blacks and white-controlled regimes in Rhodesia (Zimbabwe) and Namibia even though Moscow evinced reservations about the merits of such a course.[68]

Even at the end of the 1970s, then, the restrictions on the Soviet role in sub-Saharan Africa were numerous and varied in character. In the aggregate, they took on fairly formidable proportions.

2

Moscow's Purposes in the 1980s

Since the end of the 1970s, Soviet involvement in sub-Saharan Africa has not altered a lot. Some developments of consequence, to be sure, have taken place. Moscow has succeeded in widening its political contacts with a fair number of states in the region that had long manifested appreciable reserve toward it. During 1981, for example, the USSR exchanged parliamentary delegations with Zaire for the first time, and that same year, CPSU officials signed an accord with the ruling United National Independence Party of Zambia to establish interparty links. After Flight Lieutenant Jerry Rawlings in early 1982 seized power in Ghana for the second time in two years, Soviet-Ghanaian ties in the economic and technical spheres expanded substantially. Moscow has also made modest strides toward recouping its losses in certain states where it had suffered reversals in recent years. For instance, the USSR has managed to work out various sorts of interchanges with the new governments of Uganda and Equatorial Guinea, and it finally opened up diplomatic relations with Robert Mugabe's government in Zimbabwe in early 1981. At the same time, Soviet relations with some old friends in the area have deteriorated. Guinea provides a good illustration. Unhappy with the level of Soviet economic aid and with the results of Conakry's arrangement with the USSR for exploiting Guinean bauxite, Sékou Touré has looked increasingly westward.[69] In the economic sphere, Soviet authorities have concluded agreements with both Angola and Mozambique on long-range economic and trade cooperation – i.e., to 1990. These umbrella agreements have led to some major new Soviet commitments of a concrete nature, particularly in Angola's case. In September 1982, the USSR and Angola signed contracts for a complex of projects in Malanje Province amounting to some $400 million. Among them were a hydropower station on the Cuanza River that would double the aggregate amount of Angola's power-generating facilities, and a nearby dam that would create a large water reservoir to irrigate more than 400 thousand hectares of land.[70] Deliveries of Soviet arms would appear to have risen in the early 1980s as compared with the late 1970s, although it remains unclear whether this increase reflects a cyclical phenomenon or something more permanent.[71] At the same time, the USSR has employed its own military forces with greater frequency in support of governments friendly to it in the area. After South Africa raided the facilities of the exile African National Congress (ANC) in Matola in January 1981, for example, Soviet military vessels from the Indian Ocean visited Mozambique to show solidarity with the FRELIMO regime. Similarly, a Soviet naval task group called at Victoria, Seychelles, in late 1981 after an abortive coup against France Albert René's government there.[72]

Yet these changes have all been at the margins. They have not significantly modified the Soviet role in sub-Saharan Africa, in either a negative or a positive sense.

Such a situation, however, will not necessarily persist throughout the remainder of the 1980s. Whether it does or not will depend upon the nature of the goals that Soviet leaders choose to pursue in the region, the opportunities that the area affords Moscow, the constraints under which the USSR must function in the region, and the degree of Soviet will to exploit the available opportunities there. This chapter focuses on the first of these factors — Moscow's likely ends in sub-Saharan Africa.

Current Soviet Objectives

In approaching this issue, it is essential to begin with an assessment of the USSR's objectives in the region as of the early 1980s. Rarely if ever, of course, does Moscow announce its goals in any context; therefore, they have to be inferred from various types of Soviet behavior. But Soviet behavior is sometimes ambiguous in import. Thus, any discussion of Soviet purposes in sub-Saharan Africa entails an element of hypothesis as well as fact. This caveat, however, does not render it impossible to say something meaningful on the subject.

At the outset, it should be pointed out that the general character of Soviet goals in sub-Saharan Africa today reflects the region's specific attributes. The area contains no state that constitutes an actual or potential rival of the USSR on a global scale. It lies sufficiently distant from the USSR's borders to have no direct link to Soviet security considerations. And it possesses no resources vital to the USSR. Consequently, from the Soviet standpoint the region is basically an arena in which to pursue ends that transcend the local setting.

Four such objectives seem to underlie Soviet activities in sub-Saharan Africa at the moment:

(1) *To gain local acceptance of a lasting Soviet political, economic, and even military presence in the region.* In the early 1970s, Soviet leaders revived the claim made prema-

turely by Nikita Khrushchev in the 1950s that the USSR is a global power. As they are obviously well aware, such status does not flow from divine right or the consent of the international community; rather, it must be self-asserted, self-achieved, and self-sustained.[73] For any country to validate a claim of this sort, moreover, it must demonstrate its global reach. Such a task usually requires not just intermittent forays into distant regions but a sustained presence in those regions, and establishing this kind of presence in any given area is greatly facilitated by the cooperation of local governments.

Soviet leaders give ample signs that they understand this fact. Moscow continually strives to conclude kinds of agreements with the black-ruled states of sub-Saharan Africa that would bring Soviet personnel into the area, and it even tries to get their acquiescence to strictly Soviet military undertakings such as the calling of Soviet warships at local ports and the use of local airfields by Soviet planes for purposes of reconnaissance. It is in this same broad framework that Moscow encourages radicalization of sub-Saharan Africa. The setbacks that the USSR encountered in the mid-1960s in countries such as Ghana have left Soviet analysts highly dubious about the chances of any "genuinely" revolutionary breakthroughs in the region; hence, they display reservations about the credentials of the self-styled Marxist-Leninist regimes there.[74] Nevertheless, Soviet officials have been acutely conscious that the USSR has increased its presence in sub-Saharan Africa because of the rise to power of radical black governments in countries like Angola, Mozambique, and Ethiopia, and Soviet commentaries suggest that Moscow expects similar political transitions in the region to produce comparable results.[75]

(2) *To obtain a voice in the affairs of sub-Saharan Africa.* As just noted, Soviet authorities now loudly proclaim that the USSR is a global power. But Moscow clearly recognizes that such proclamations will have no substance unless the

USSR actually exercises influence around the world, and it seeks to help shape events in even the remotest corners of the globe. More than a decade ago, for example, Soviet Foreign Minister Andrei Gromyko insisted that "today there is no question of any significance which can be decided without the Soviet Union or in opposition to it."[76] In this context, then, the USSR has a big stake in making its weight felt in sub-Saharan Africa.

At the moment, the regional issue whose outcome Soviet leaders try hardest to affect is the racial conflict in Southern Africa. Moscow regularly denounces the Afrikaner government of South Africa for racist policies in Nambia as well as in South Africa proper, and it backs the stance of African countries against the seating of that government in the UN General Assembly. The USSR maintains close relations with the most important militant internal foe of the Afrikaner government — the ANC. Similarly, it furnishes the bulk of the weapons and equipment of SWAPO, the national liberation movement waging a guerrilla struggle in Namibia. Moscow even serves as the main arms supplier to many of the frontline states of Southern Africa, including Angola, Zambia, and Mozambique.

(3) *To weaken, though not to eradicate, the Western position in sub-Saharan Africa.* From Moscow's perspective, the USSR is engaged in a competition with the West for influence in the region, and this competition is a zero-sum game. That is, gains for one side entail losses for the other side.[77] In such a framework, Western influence must decrease for the Soviet role in the area to grow.

At the same time, Moscow believes that a precipitate departure by the West from sub-Saharan Africa would prove undesirable from the Soviet standpoint. As it has noted in a more general context, "the Soviet Union's potential for rendering economic assistance is not infinite," and "of course, the Soviet Union cannot fail to be concerned for the well-being of its own people."[78] Thus, Soviet observers now recog-

nize the need for a long-range strategy to bring about industrialization of sub-Saharan Africa and other Third World
areas along socialist lines. Moreover, even the more conservative among Soviet analysts suggest that "socialist-oriented
states" in the Third World should not shun Western capital
but seek to attract it by establishing rules that offer foreign
investors advantages that do not damage local interests.[79]

(4) *To limit, and wherever possible reduce, Chinese influence in sub-Saharan Africa.* Beijing's stature in the region has
declined since the 1975–1976 Angolan civil war because of
its inability to affect the outcome of that conflict positively
for its Angolan clients, but Moscow still regards China as
a threat to the USSR's efforts to establish itself as the chief
patron of national liberation and revolutionary movements
there as well as in the rest of Africa.[80] In 1982, to be sure,
the Chinese for the first time in many years began to show
a real desire to effect some sort of rapprochement with the
Soviets. Nevertheless, Beijing made clear that it did not pro-
pose to abandon its challenge to Moscow in the Third World.
Indeed, Premier Zhao Ziyang's extended trip to North and
sub-Saharan Africa in December 1982 and January 1983
underscored Chinese resolve to assert a role for itself there.
Not since the mid-1960s had a Chinese premier engaged in
such travels on the African continent. In such a context, the
Soviet struggle with China for influence in sub-Saharan
Africa also takes on the features of a zero-sum game.

Possible Changes

This set of objectives, of course, is not fixed in concrete, and
it could undergo modification in the years ahead. Such a shift
in goals, however, would necessitate Moscow's redefinition
or reordering of the interests that it perceives for the USSR
in sub-Saharan Africa.[81]

Although it is not totally inconceivable that Soviet leaders might discern new interests for the USSR in the region in the future, this sort of development seems relatively unlikely. Far more probable would be a revision of the individual priorities that Moscow now attaches to its perceived interests. In this context, it is important to keep in mind that the interests that a state sees for itself are not always harmonious or complementary. In fact, interests vis-à-vis a specific geographic area may conflict with one another and interests with respect to that area often compete with those related to other areas. This is especially true for states that regard themselves as global powers and set forth their interests in worldwide terms. Thus, a state at any given time may have to pursue some of its interests at the expense of others.

There have been indications that Moscow perceives three Soviet interests in sub-Saharan Africa aside from those that the USSR is currently trying to satisfy. Were Soviet leaders to opt to alter the present mix of their operational objectives, it is these interests that would in all likelihood find reflection in the changes. Therefore, they bear scrutiny.

The first of these perceived interests is the transition of the countries of the region to "genuine" socialism. Soviet media constantly reiterate that such a transition will come about eventually in all Third World areas, and they suggest that it will strengthen not only the socialist camp in general but the USSR in particular as the core element of the camp. Furthermore, although promoting "real" socialist transformations has not figured in Soviet activities in sub-Saharan Africa in recent years, it did do so earlier in the post-independence period. From the late 1950s until the mid-1960s, optimism about the revolutionary potential of at least some portions of the area ran high in Moscow, and Soviet leaders tried to encourage the emergence of full-fledged Communist states in those cases.[82]

A second perceived interest is guaranteeing access to the minerals of sub-Saharan Africa – not so much for the USSR itself as for its fellow members of CMEA, particularly those in Eastern Europe. As is well known, the region has rich endowments of a variety of minerals. These include oil, platinum, chromium, cobalt, vanadium, gold, manganese, fluorspar, diamonds, nickel, uranium, zinc, phosphate, asbestos, antimony, lead, iron ore, coal, titanium, copper, quartz, alabaster, and silicate. South Africa alone boasts the largest reserves of platinum, chromium, vanadium, gold, manganese, and fluorspar of any country in the world. It also ranks second in reserves of diamonds; third in reserves of nickel; fourth in reserves of uranium, zinc, and phosphate; fifth in reserves of asbestos, antimony, and lead; sixth in reserves of iron ore and coal; eighth in reserves of titanium; and tenth in reserves of copper.[83]

Soviet commentaries about the area's minerals have invariably stressed the West's alleged designs on them and have avoided any hint of a Soviet concern with them. Nevertheless, the commentaries have revealed a clear understanding of their magnitude,[84] and this is sufficient to make them of considerable relevance to Moscow's endeavors to cope with some problems that loom on the horizon for the USSR. Although the USSR itself possesses enough reserves of the minerals that sub-Saharan Africa has to offer to render it essentially self-sufficient, claims on Soviet output of such minerals do not stem just from domestic demand. The USSR is also the chief supplier of these minerals for other CMEA members, especially the East European states. As of the early 1980s, however, the USSR has already had difficulty in meeting CMEA needs for oil, and the likelihood that it will encounter increasing problems in this realm as the decade progresses appears high. Similar situations could arise in the near future with respect to other minerals as well.[85] These sorts of circumstances make the USSR desire to ensure the availability of sub-Saharan Africa's minerals to itself and its allies.

The final perceived Soviet interest is impeding Western access to the minerals of sub-Saharan Africa and disrupting Western use of the sea lanes that lie around much of the region. As just mentioned, the area is a storehouse of minerals, and these mineral resources plainly have significance for the West. For example, the region constitutes the major non-Communist source of supply of a number of minerals important to the West's advanced industrial economies – cobalt, chromium, platinum, and manganese.[86] The area's sea lanes possess no less weight in the eyes of the West. More than half of Western Europe's imports of oil and about 20 percent of those of the United States travel through part of these waters on their way from the Persian Gulf to their ultimate destination.[87] Moreover, the key water route between the Mediterranean Sea and the Indian Ocean, via the Suez Canal and the Red Sea, passes by the countries of the Horn and through the critical choke point of the Strait of Bab el-Mandeb. Of such facts, Moscow is acutely aware. Indeed, Soviet commentaries have harped on them – always with the implication that they reflect Western vulnerabilities.[88]

Conclusions

Although Soviet leaders at some juncture in the 1980s could decide to translate these discerned interests into operational goals, the chances that they will actually do so appear fairly slim for a combination of reasons. One of these is the inhibitions that the record of the current set of Soviet objectives vis-à-vis sub-Saharan Africa generates. Not only has the USSR pursued these ends without major modifications for roughly two decades, but by limiting its operational goals to this particular mix of ends and persistently working to realize them, it has managed to make substantial progress toward accomplishing each. Such advances produce a reluctance to alter a successful formula. For example, Soviet officials in recent years have often hinted that when the USSR in the past allowed itself to become overly optimistic about what could be achieved in several places in the region, it suffered bitter disappointments.[89]

To override this consideration would require a compelling argument of some kind. Although it would be foolish to rule out the possibility of the emergence of such an argument at some juncture over the rest of the decade, none seems to exist at the moment.

However attractive Moscow might find the transition of at least some countries of sub-Saharan Africa to "true" socialism, it clearly does not see this development as looming on the near horizon. As pointed out earlier, Soviet analysts have consistently described the self-styled Marxist-Leninist states of the region as "revolutionary democracies with vangard parties," and they have suggested that much remains to be done there before these countries acquire Marxist-Leninist status in Soviet eyes. In the 1980s, the USSR has even reduced the level of its attention to such states in its overall foreign policy toward the area.[90]

Although Moscow may have a concern about insuring access for the USSR and its CMEA allies to the minerals of sub-Saharan Africa, it displays no evident sense of urgency about the matter. Its relaxed attitude no doubt reflects the generally positive situation that confronts it at present. Aside from oil, it can still satisfy the mineral needs of its allies with relative ease. Even if that state of affairs changed unexpectedly, the USSR now enjoys good political and economic access to all of the countries of sub-Saharan Africa with minerals except South Africa and Namibia, and many of its

CMEA allies—particularly the GDR, which is the most highly dependent on Soviet supplies of any of the East European countries—have moved to position themselves in a similar fashion.[91] The only impediment to acquiring minerals from the region, then, lies in the problem of paying for them.

No matter how much Moscow might like to deny the West access to sub-Saharan Africa's minerals or to disrupt Western use of the sea lanes around a lot of the region, the USSR at the moment does not possess the capabilities to do either, and any attempt to remedy this deficiency will require considerable time and effort. As for the area's minerals, the countries that sell these to the West must export their resources to carry out their own development programs. Therefore, they are not likely to yield to mere political exhortations to cut off Western supplies.[92] Yet the USSR does not offer an alternative market for these minerals. As we have seen and as Soviet analysts themselves concede, the share of sub-Saharan African states and the USSR in each other's overall trade has stayed exceedingly small.[93] In light of the USSR's own economic problems and its need for imports of advanced technology to help deal with these, Moscow probably has little chance of altering this circumstance significantly by the end of the decade.

With respect to the sea lanes, it is true that the USSR now has some naval forces operating in or near these waters. As noted previously, the USSR permanently maintains a task force in the Indian Ocean off the east coast of Africa and a smaller patrol along the west coast of the continent. These forces also enjoy access to different types of facilities in the Dahlak Islands, in Aden, and in Socotra—all close to the Strait of Bab el-Mandeb—and pay port calls at a wide number of cities in sub-Saharan Africa, among them Lagos, Nigeria; Luanda, Angola; Victoria, Seychelles; and Maputo and Beira, Mozambique.[94]

Nevertheless, Moscow could hardly mount a credible campaign to disrupt the sea lanes on the basis of such assets. Although theoretically Soviet leaders might deploy additional forces to reinforce the existing ones, there would still be massive logistical problems, and the USSR would probably require the use of more facilities in the area than those to which it has access at present.[95] Meeting this requirement would pose great difficulties — especially since local governments could wind up involving themselves in a casus belli with the West by extending such privileges. In fact, these difficulties would probably prove insurmountable unless Moscow succeeded in depicting its campaign as compatible with the interests of local governments.

On balance, then, Soviet objectives in sub-Saharan Africa appear unlikely to alter much during the rest of the 1980s. If modifications take place in the USSR's role in the region over these years, they will probably have to come from other influences.

3

Soviet Opportunities in the 1980s

Any estimate of future opportunities for the USSR in sub-Saharan Africa must explicitly recognize at the outset the limitations of the undertaking. Such an estimate has to rest largely upon projection of current trends and developments. Thus, it inevitably downplays the impact of aberrant events that could significantly change the openings available to Moscow. For this reason, the estimate can only be probabilistic, not predictive, in nature.

Even so, it would seem that the USSR will clearly enjoy substantial opportunities throughout the remainder of the decade to enhance its role in the region. The factors that contribute to this state of affairs fall into four general categories: political, economic, racial, and military.

Political Conditions

In the political realm, there has been a rise in internal instability in most countries of the region during recent years. This instability has multiple roots.

Mass popular movements have nearly disappeared from the independent countries of sub-Saharan Africa, and ruling groups almost everywhere in the area now have limited social and political bases. Nevertheless, these ruling groups typically couch their particularistic interests in terms of "national interest." As a consequence, they encourage other groups with no less valid claims to reflect the "national interest" to challenge them. The inevitable result has been growing political fragmentation and heightened political conflict. Chad affords perhaps the most extreme example to date. As of the early 1980s, 11 different political factions have emerged in this state of fewer than 5 million people, and the country verges constantly on civil war. Indeed, it has experienced intermittent outbreaks of heavy armed fighting over the last few years.

The widespread lack of political institutions that could serve to aggregate interests and to channel political competition along constructive lines enhances the potential for upheaval inherent in these circumstances. A good illustration of this deficiency is the prevalence of one-party, nonparty authoritarian, and white-minority political systems. Most states to which the colonial authorities bequeathed multi- or two-party systems have since discarded them. Only in Botswana, Gambia, Mauritius, and Zimbabwe do these legacies persist today. Moreover, Gambia and Zimbabwe cling only tenuously to their inheritances. Indeed, President Mugabe of Zimbabwe has expressed a desire to establish a one-party system in his country by the mid-1980s. Nigeria, Senegal, and Uganda, to be sure, have now reinstituted multiparty systems after extended periods of one-party or military government, but the verdict is still out on how lasting these systems will prove to be. Ghana's checkered history since the early 1960s dictates caution in reaching judgments on this score. Although there have been two attempts to restore a multiparty system in Ghana, neither effort survived more than about two years. Aside from these seven states, single-party, nonparty authoritarian, or white-minority rule prevails throughout the region. In a few cases like Tanzania, it is true, governing elements have endeavored to foster some political competition and the expression of opposition within these systems; however, such undertakings have been exceptional, not characteristic.

A further complication lies in the fragility of existing political institutions in many places. Although the bulk of the countries of the region have rejected the political institutions that the colonial powers passed on to them, a local concensus has often failed to develop as to the appropriate political forms to be adopted. Thus, a sizable number of states have lurched from one type of government to another in fairly rapid succession. Uganda, for example, has moved from a multiparty system to a single-party system to a military dictatorship and now back to a multiparty system in the space of two decades. Even where political institutions have enjoyed some degree of longevity, this has not infrequently reflected the dominant role of an aging founding father, and whether the institutions over which these individuals have presided will now survive them remains an open question. Although Kenya, Botswana, Senegal, and Mauritius have already gone through transitions from the rule of such founding fathers without major changes in political forms, these transitions took place so recently that their long-term effects have not yet had a chance to become visible. Furthermore, similar transitions still loom on the near horizon in countries like the Ivory Coast and Lesotho.

In light of the narrow social foundations of most sub-Saharan African governments, it is hardly surprising that efforts at state consolidation have also exacerbated ethnic and cultural divisions in a lot of countries. Burundi offers a good illustration. The minority Tutsi have long held the reins of power in the country, but their attempts to solidify their position and ensure their continued control have tended to enlarge the gulf between them and the majority Hutus. Tensions arising from a heightened sense of "separate" identity, in turn, make political bargaining and compromise difficult. Finally, corruption has become so blatant and pervasive among the political elite in some countries as to stir grass roots discontent. The temptation to exploit public office for personal gain is by no means one to which sub-Saharan Africans are peculiarly prone to succumb. Indeed, even officials in Communist states fall prey to it. Nonetheless, the scale and conspicuousness of corrupt activities has plainly been on the increase in many places in the region in recent years. These may have reached unprecedented heights in the Central African Empire of Jean-Bédel Bokassa and the Uganda of Idi Amin Dada in the late 1970s, but they are still impressive in countries like Zaire even today. More important, the scope of illicit activities and the open flaunting of wealth gleaned from them have evoked strong popular resentment — especially in those countries where the general population has faced severe economic hardships. Such resentment played a part in the military coups that brought Master Sergeant Samuel Doe and Flight Lieutenant Jerry Rawlings to power in Liberia and Ghana, respectively, in the early 1980s.

It is most improbable that these conditions will alter much in the near future, so domestic political instability seems destined to stay at fairly high levels in sub-Saharan Africa throughout the 1980s. This state of affairs will have special relevance for the USSR in two respects. First, political instability could lead to radicalization of the governments of some countries, through changes of rulers or shifts in the attitudes of rulers. Indeed, such a process has occurred in a number of places in the region over the last decade or so and has ultimately redounded to Moscow's advantage. Ethiopia and Benin constitute two cases in point. Second, competing groups within specific countries could seek allies abroad to further their causes. The tendency toward "internationalization" of internal strife has become quite pronounced during recent years, and there is no reason to expect it to disappear in the years ahead.

Along with the mounting of domestic political instability has gone an increase in interstate discord. This heightened discord stems from a combination of factors.

At least the dominant elements in most sub-Saharan African countries have displayed growing identification with their "states," and that identification has produced not only a commitment to preserve those states but often a desire to strengthen them. Such attitudes, while positive for the highly heterogeneous societies of the region in the sense that outlooks of this kind represent the expansion of loyalties beyond the confines of the tribe and other particularistic groups to more general entities, have tended to make dealings between governments more acrimonious than was previously the case. Indeed, they have especially complicated the task of settling quarrels over boundaries left from colonial days. The course of relations between Kenya and Somalia in recent years provides a prime illustration. These relations, uneasy since the 1960s as a result of Somalia's claims on Kenya's northeast territories, deteriorated greatly in the wake of the Mogadishu goverment's attempt to wrest the Ogaden region from Ethiopia by force in 1977. This abortive effort caused the conservative government in Nairobi to make common international cause with the revolutionary military regime in Addis Ababa, the arch enemy of Somalia.

In addition, the inhibitions that most sub-Saharan African rulers once showed about interfering in the politics of other countries in the region have diminished. Meddling in the affairs of other states is not a new phenomenon in the area. Prior to his overthrow in 1966, for instance, Kwame Nkrumah of Ghana operated several camps to train dissi-

dents from a number of sub-Saharan African countries—
especially Ghana's neighbors—in techniques of subversion
and guerrilla warfare.[96] As governments with narrow political and social bases have become more and more common in
the region, however, the practice has assumed a widespread
character. Even such a staunch defender of African sovereignty as Julius Nyerere of Tanzania has succumbed to it.
After Idi Amin Dada seized power in Uganda in the early
1970s, Tanzania gave shelter to many of his opponents, and
it went so far as to help mount a military force to unseat him
at the end of the decade.

The prospects for significant reversal of either of these
tendencies appear dim for the short and medium term. Perhaps more critical, no highly effective mechanism for control-
ling their impact exists. The OAU came into being in 1963
with quite limited powers, and while it has made major contributions to the dampening of some international conflicts
such as the one growing out of the civil war in Chad in the
1980s, its overall record as an instrumentality for dealing
with interstate strife remains spotty. Nor does the area offer
a good candidate to serve as regional mediator. In terms of
size and resources, Nigeria and South Africa have the greatest
potential in this regard. However, Nigeria still has enough
domestic political and economic problems to keep its attention focused largely on internal matters for some time to
come, while South Africa is a pariah state and will continue
to be one until Pretoria's white-minority government works
out an accommodation with the country's black majority.

A high level of interstate discord, then, will probably persist in the area throughout the rest of the 1980s. This discord
will in all likelihood afford the USSR substantial openings
in the region. In recent years, sub-Saharan African countries
have evinced a strong disposition to look for political backing outside the continent in their quarrels with one another,

and many have turned to Moscow in particular. There seem little grounds to believe that this inclination will change in the foreseeable future.

Economic Trends

In the economic sphere, virtually all the states in sub-Saharan Africa have experienced severe difficulties in recent years. To grasp the exact import of these difficulties, it is crucial to bear in mind some fundamental aspects of the region. Sub-Saharan Africa contains 20 of the 30 countries that the United Nations Conference on Trade and Development has classified as the least developed in the world.[97] Moreover, of the 48 political entities in the area (including Namibia, South Africa, and the offshore island states), only South Africa, Zimbabwe, Nigeria, and Zaire can boast of significant industrial capacity at present.[98] No less important, the estimated gross national incomes per capita in 1981 for 26 of the countries in the region were $400 or less, and those for 14 other countries ran between $400 and $800. Thus, in just 8 cases did the figures exceed $800. Those for 2 countries fell between $800 and $1,000, while the rest topped $1,000.[99] Furthermore, the available evidence on income distribution in the area suggests that the figures for these 8 entities may convey a somewhat misleading picture of their basic economic conditions. Although a high degree of inequality in the distribution of incomes may be found in individual countries with GNPs per capita below $800 – for example, Liberia and Zaire – this seems to be typical of those with GNPs per capita in excess of that amount. Relevant data exist for five of the eight countries in the latter category. In the case of Gabon, the top 5 percent of the earning population receives 45.3 percent of the national income, while the bottom 20 percent receives 3.2 percent of it. For Mauritius, the figures are 45 percent and 4.5

percent, respectively; and for the Ivory Coast, 30 percent and 4 percent. In South Africa, whites, who constitute less than 20 percent of the total population, earn five times as much as blacks, who make up 70 percent of the population. The disparity is even more pronounced in Namibia. Whites, who comprise slightly more than 10 percent of the population, get about $2,300 a year, while blacks, who account for more than 80 percent of the population, receive about $130 a year.[100]

In such a context, even minor problems can have far-reaching ramifications, and the problems that have emerged in sub-Saharan Africa since the early 1970s certainly qualify as something more than minor in character. Most countries in the region, for example, have failed to achieve sufficient economic growth to keep pace with the rising expectations of their populations. During 1970–1980, 26 of the 48 political entities there recorded negative rates of average annual real growth of gross domestic product (GDP) per capita, and another eight had rates of less than 2 percent. Thus, only 14 countries registered rates of average annual real growth of GDP per capita that were higher than 2 percent. Of these, six chalked up rates between 2 and 4 percent; another seven between 4 and 7 percent. Gabon offered the prime success story in the area, with a rate of 10.4 percent.[101]

Failure to produce enough food to meet the basic requirements of a rapidly expanding population has in many instances exacerbated the impact of poor overall economic performance. It has even become a matter of concern for some countries with at least moderately good rates of general economic growth. During the 1970s, 26 of the 39 sub-Saharan African states for which data exist had average annual rates of increase in volume of food production that ran below the average yearly rates of growth of their populations, and in 14 cases—Angola, Chad, Congo, Ethiopia, Gabon, Gambia, Ghana, Guinea, Mali, Mauritania, Mozambique, Senegal, Somalia, and Togo—the difference was quite a large one. Only seven countries – Cameroon, Ivory Coast, Liberia, Malawi, Rwanda, Sudan, and Swaziland – turned in reasonably decent performances in this regard. As a consequence, the annual rate of growth of food imports for the states of the region escalated. For instance, that for commercial imports of cereal rose from 9.0 percent at the beginning of the period to 9.5 percent at its end.[102]

To a considerable degree, the food situation relates directly to another problem. Over the years, all but a few governments in the area (those of the Ivory Coast and Malawi constitute notable exceptions) have tended to regard industrialization, rather than the expansion of agricultural output, as the key to long-term economic development, but industrialization has not thus far yielded many of the benefits expected of it. Although many sub-Saharan African states now have at least the beginnings of a modern industrial sector, this sector typically constitutes a burden on agriculture, not a support of it. To create such a sector, most governments have accorded industry priority of claim to scarce foreign exchange, and this policy has deprived the agricultural sector of some essential inputs – especially of a technological nature – to improve production. Moreover, the industrial undertakings launched have not generated the capital for investment in other, including agricultural, projects that it was anticipated they would, for protectionist policies on the part of most governments have rendered the productivity of these enterprises low and hence the costs of their output high. Nor has development of an industrial sector even laid a sound foundation for further industrial growth in many cases. A large proportion of the new industrial ventures are import intensive. That is, they rely heavily upon inputs from abroad instead of local raw materials and labor. This is especially the case for oil-extracting enterprises. Such operations, therefore, do not stimulate much additional activity in the rest of the economy.[103]

Except for South Africa and for the oil-exporting states of Angola, Congo, Gabon, and Nigeria, the countries of sub-Saharan Africa since the early 1970s have also faced a pronounced and consistent worsening of their balance of payments, and a large percentage of them have run deficits during many years. For the region's oil-importing states as a group, the deficits have averaged 9 percent of their annual gross domestic products – a figure twice that for all oil-importing countries and conspicuously higher than that for any other region of the world. Such a situation reflects a mix of influences. With the increasing gap between their food production and the growth of their populations, a number of countries have had to buy food – or, in some instances, additional food – from abroad. Furthermore, the cost of some imports has risen significantly. The real price of oil, for example, jumped fivefold during the 1970s. At the same time, exporters of minerals, particularly copper and iron ore, have confronted a strong downward trend in world market prices for their commodities. Perhaps most important, the pace of growth of the exports of these countries has slowed. Of the 26 countries for which information is available, 22 recorded a lower rate of export growth during the 1970s than during the 1900s, moreover, 17 of them chalked up negative rates of export growth during the 1970s, as compared with only one of them during the 1960s.[104]

Although the countries that have experienced the deficits have succeeded in offsetting them in part through development assistance from official donors, this approach has not sufficed to take care of the difficulty since the mid-1970s. Thus, these states have had to resort to depleting their foreign exchange reserves and to expanding their borrowing sharply. By 1979, the reserves of this group as a whole had dropped to an amount required to cover imports for about two months, and the figure had fallen even lower by the early 1980s. As a consequence of the swelling of the group's external debt, the debt-service ratio for all the region's oil importers (that is, their interest and amortization payments as a percentage of their export earnings) climbed from about 6 percent in 1970 to 12.4 percent in 1979. Indeed, six of the countries even had to renegotiate their multilateral loans.[105] The 1980s have witnessed a worsening of the situation in this regard. Between the beginning of 1980 and the close of 1982, no less than 12 states had to reschedule their debt payments to either commercial or multilateral lenders.[106]

The resolution of problems of such dimensions will obviously not take place overnight, so they are likely to continue to plague sub-Saharan Africa to some extent for the remainder of the decade. This state of affairs will probably affect the USSR's opportunities in the region in both indirect and direct ways: In the former respect, it will contribute to political instability in the area and thereby enhance the chances for political developments favorable to Moscow. In the latter, it will provide openings for Soviet leaders to exploit through various types of trade and aid.

Racial Tensions

Racially-based hostility has reached new heights in sub-Saharan Africa since the mid-1970s. Paradoxically, this development has reflected the accumulating successes of black "liberation" forces in the region.

During the 1950s and 1960s, the decisions of Britain, France, Belgium, and ultimately Spain to dissolve their empires and to transfer power in their sub-Saharan African colonies to the black majorities of these territories kept racial animosity in the area at a moderately low level. To be sure, armed struggle by black liberation movements got under way in most of the African colonies of recalcitrant Portugal in the early 1960s, and a similar development took place in Rhodesia (now Zimbabwe) after the white minority there unilaterally declared the colony's independence in 1965, and in Namibia after South Africa defied the UN dissolution of Pretoria's League of Nations mandate over the territory in 1966. In addition, the black liberation movements in South Africa forsook the path of nonviolence in the 1960s as a consequence of the repression carried out by the Afrikaner government in the wake of the 1960 Sharpeville demonstrations. Yet the progress toward sovereignty being made elsewhere tended to preoccupy blacks in the region. Moreover, the guerrilla efforts of most of the armed liberation movements did not yield spectacular advances even into the 1970s. Thus, the vast majority of whites in the countries that they still controlled remained convinced that their rule would endure indefinitely.

Circumstances began to change in the early 1970s with the end of the transitions to independence in the great bulk of the former British, French, Belgian, and Spanish colonies in sub-Saharan Africa. Now both these new and the older states in the area focused their attention more intensely on places still under white domination. The key event that transformed the situation, however, was the April 1974 coup in Lisbon. This soon led to the demise of the Portuguese empire in Africa, and especially to the breach of the white redoubt of Southern Africa through the emergence of black governments in Mozambique and Angola.

As a result of such developments, the attitudes of both blacks and whites in sub-Saharan Africa underwent profound shifts. Blacks, for their part, interpreted the collapse of the Portuguese empire as an indication that the end of white rule everywhere in the region loomed on the not-too-distant horizon. More salient, they concluded that increased violence offered the best method of bringing down the remaining white-minority governments in the shortest possible time. They recognized, of course, that the Portuguese colonies had not won sovereignty through military takeovers by local black liberation movements; however, they deemed that armed struggle by blacks had played a decisive role in sapping the political will of the Portuguese to hold on to power. As far as whites in the few countries left under white control were concerned, they tended to react with alarm to the transfer of authority to the black majorities in the former Portuguese colonies. Not only did they evince a mounting sense of political vulnerability, but they manifested fears of losing their privileged economic positions as well. The almost inevitable outcome was an escalation of racial hostility in the area, particularly in Zimbabwe and Namibia.

Nor has the negotiated settlement of the war in Zimbabwe and the installation of a black government there under Robert Mugabe in 1980 gone far to dampen the tensions. Mugabe's call for reconciliation between the races in Zimbabwe has made a positive impression on some whites in the country and elsewhere in Southern Africa. In fact, several white members of parliament in Zimbabwe have now departed from Ian Smith's Rhodesian Front because of its continuing intransigent opposition to the new government. Resolution of the Zimbabwe situation by peaceful means has also spurred Western efforts, under the auspices of the United Nations, to produce a peaceful settlement in Namibia, and these could yield positive results across the longer term. At the same time, the elimination of white domination in Zimbabwe has stiffened the determination of blacks in sub-Saharan Africa to press ahead aggressively with respect to Namibia and South Africa. They now have a strong belief that the momentum of events is in their favor. Yet today they confront the most formidable barrier to the achievement of their goals that they have faced thus far—the white minority in South Africa. Because the South African government still retains final authority in Namibia, it is this group that holds the key to what happens even there.

The response of white South Africans to developments

in Southern Africa in the late 1970s and early 1980s has been complex. They have almost universally displayed a beleaguered feeling, but they have differed significantly about how to approach the challenge that lies before them. There has been rising sentiment – among Afrikaners as well as non-Afrikaners – for political change and some form of accommodation with blacks.[107] However, few of such a persuasion would go so far as to accept black-majority rule. Other whites endorse only cosmetic alterations in the status quo. They see no harm in doing away with social and economic irritants to blacks, such as inferior education and bars to skilled jobs, but they draw the line at any type of concession in the political sphere. Still other whites oppose any type of modification of the present systems in Namibia or South Africa. This group has hardened its stand during the 1980s. For example, 16 members of the South African parliament split from the ruling Nationalist Party and formed a new Conservative Party in early 1982 on the issue of extending the vote to coloreds (persons of mixed racial ancestry) and Indians.

In light of the divisions within white and particularly Afrikaner ranks, the Pretoria government has attempted to steer a course that embodies contradictory elements. Domestically, it has eased or eliminated some aspects of the apartheid system, but it has continued to push for the formal creation of so-called black homelands and to repress black political expression and organizational activity that does not conform to its guidelines. Externally, it has conducted negotiations with the Western powers on the future of Namibia; however, it has not hesitated to conduct forays into neighboring states to knock out facilities it deems threatening and to strike blows against exile forces of its black opposition. Such policies have served to raise serious questions among blacks throughout sub-Saharan Africa about the good faith of its positive moves. Thus, these steps have failed to have any visible impact on racial animosity in the region.

Whatever the outcome of the current negotiations on the

fate of Namibia, the problems of South Africa are complicated enough that they are most unlikely to vanish even by
the close of the 1980s. Therefore, racial tensions in sub-Saharan Africa will probably not diminish a great deal, if at all,
over the rest of the decade. They could even heighten.
This state of affairs holds considerable potential for exploitation by the USSR. Although Soviet relations with sub-
Saharan Africa have not been devoid of what black Africans
perceive as racial prejudice, Moscow has long attempted to
project itself as the champion of anti-imperialism and anti-
racism in the region, and that posture has increasingly left
its mark on the attitudes toward the USSR of blacks in the
area. In contrast, the Western powers, especially the United
States and Great Britain, have tended to be viewed as am-
bivalent and equivocal on racial matters by many blacks of
sub-Saharan Africa. Particularly with respect to South Africa, they are deemed to have let strategic considerations and
economic investments temper their stands on the principle
of racial equality.

The Military Situation

Recent years have witnessed a mounting inclination on the
part of sub-Saharan Africans to resort to the use of force to
pursue their political, economic, and social goals. In the late
1970s, for example, Idi Amin Dada of Uganda sought to com-
pel Tanzania to curtail the activities of Ugandan exiles in
Tanzania against his regime by sending his army into northern Tanzania on the pretext that the Dar es Salaam government had launched a military invasion of Uganda. President
Julius Nyerere of Tanzania then committed a substantial portion of the Tanzanian army to assist Amin's exile opponents
in toppling him from power. Although this case may constitute an extreme one, other illustrations that do not involve

the dispatch of large numbers of troops across state borders abound. Indeed, in contrast with the 1960s, the employment of force to further particular ends has now become commonplace.

The explanation of this shift in attitudes is not hard to discern. As already noted, domestic, interstate, and racial conflict has been on the rise in sub-Saharan Africa for a considerable period, and ways of resolving conflict peacefully often do not exist at present. Most internal political systems in the region exclude large portions of the local populations from any real say in the affairs of government. Even in the exceptional cases, the newness of political institutions and the absence of traditions of political compromise typically render disputes of any kind difficult to cope with. In the international domain, the OAU in most instances has had little success in bringing about settlement of strife between or among its members. Nor has any state in the area taken on the role of regional mediator.

At any rate, the upshot has been a scramble in sub-Saharan Africa to build up the capabilities to use force — whether to advance one's own purposes or to defend against military onslaught by others. A growing "militarization" of the region has resulted. Although it is impossible to quantify this trend in precise terms, there are a few statistics that can be cited to give a rough notion of its intensity.

The first set has to do with the military expenditures of governments in the area. In 1979, 20 of 35 sub-Saharan African countries for which data are available (including South Africa and Zimbabwe) devoted 2 percent or more of their gross national products to military outlays. Of the remaining 13 states, figures for 1978 are at hand for 5, and these exceeded 2 percent in 4 instances. In 7 out of the 24 cases where military expenditures consumed more than 2 percent of GNP, such outlays ran between 5 and 10 percent of GNP. This general picture differed sharply from the one at the end of the 1960s. Thirty-six of the 40 countries under consideration here had enjoyed or claimed independence by 1969. Of that 36, just 12 put more than 2 percent of their GNPs into military expenditures that year. Moreover, only 2 of the 12 channeled more than 5 percent of their GNPs into military outlays. (Three of the 4 countries that garnered independence after 1969, it should be mentioned, spent more than 2 percent of their GNPs on military expenditures in 1978 or 1979.)[108]

The other relevant statistic concerns arms transfers. During 1975-1979, the independent governments of sub-Saharan Africa (including those of South Africa and Zimbabwe) obtained $6,830 million in arms from abroad. The total for the entire 1961-1971 decade had amounted to only $1,063 million.[109]

This trend toward "militarization" has been of great significance to Moscow because hand in hand with it has gone a decreasing reluctance on the part of many sub-Saharan Africans to have military dealings with the USSR. The change in attitude has manifested itself in a variety of forms. As pointed out in Chapter 1, Soviet deliveries of military weapons and equipment to the region increased dramatically in the last half of the 1970s, and so did the degree of the area's dependence on the USSR for supplies of arms. There was even a modest expansion of the list of recipients of Soviet arms. Perhaps most telling, the MPLA of Angola accepted Soviet and Cuban military assistance to help establish itself in power in 1975-1976, and the military rulers of Ethiopia enlisted massive Soviet and Cuban military support to drive Somalia's invading forces from the Ogaden in 1977-1978.

Obviously, economic constraints will impose some limits on the scale and pace of any further "militarization" in sub-Saharan Africa in the years ahead, but the conflict and consequent insecurity endemic to the region today seem unlikely to abate greatly in the foreseeable future. In fact, they could even become more acute. Under such conditions, sub-Saharan

Africans will probably persist in seeking arms and other types of military backing and succor from outside the region throughout the remainder of the 1980s. Because black African inhibitions about military links with the USSR have clearly diminished over the last decade or so, such quests will in all likelihood afford Moscow a lot of new openings upon which it might capitalize.

4

Circumstances in Key Soviet Targets

Sub-Saharan Africa as a whole, then, will probably provide the sort of soil from which Moscow could reap impressive harvests in the 1980s. However, Soviet leaders as long ago as the early 1960s ceased trying to define exploitable Third World opportunities in broad, undifferentiated, regional terms. Over the ensuing years, they have focused, instead, on individual countries. Since the mid-1960s, moreover, they have tended to attach greater weight to openings in countries of some intrinsic and demonstrable importance from their perspective – for example, those with significant political clout in the international arena, those with major economic resources and potential, and those on territory of strategic consequence – than to openings elsewhere.[110] Therefore, the USSR's likely opportunities in sub-Saharan Africa in the 1980s need to be examined within such a framework.

Currently there would appear to be three places in the region where factors that give countries importance from the Soviet standpoint coexist with local conditions that might afford Moscow substantial room for maneuver in the years immediately ahead. These places are the Horn of Africa, Zaire, and Southern Africa.

The Horn

Because the Horn of Africa lies at one end of the transit route between the Mediterranean Sea and the Indian Ocean via the Suez Canal and the Red Sea, it has enjoyed considerable significance from a strategic viewpoint for many years. To be sure, the merits of this route between the two key bodies of water have declined somewhat since the 1960s, for the Canal has not been able to accommodate some of the large vessels that now sail the seas – especially the big tankers that transport oil. But completion of the second phase of the Canal expansion program sometime during the 1980s will render it possible for nearly all sizes of tankers to transit the canal at least one way. Furthermore, despite its existing deficiencies, the route continues to be of major importance in both commercial and military terms even at present. It should also be pointed out that whatever loss in strategic value the Horn may have suffered from the decreased utility of the Suez Canal-Red Sea route has been more than offset by the growing dependence of many countries, particularly the industrialized states, on oil from the Persian Gulf. The Horn is quite close to the outlet of the Persian Gulf; hence, it could serve as a base from which to launch an effort to cut off the flow of oil from the Gulf.

Moscow has long recognized these strategic virtues of the Horn. Indeed, serious Soviet attention to the Horn began in the late 1950s, with courtship of Ethiopia. Emperor Haile Selassie, however, merely flirted with the USSR to make the United States, Ethiopia's international patron, more receptive to his requests for arms and assurances of U.S. interest in the country's territorial integrity; he remained wedded to the U.S. tie essentially up to the time of his desposal in 1974. Thus, Moscow in the 1960s turned to the Eritrean "liberation" movement and, more important, to Somalia to try to establish a measure of influence in the Horn.

Soviet efforts in the latter case bore fruit of real consequence, especially after Colonel (later Major General) Mohamed Siad Barre seized power in Mogadishu in October 1969. By the early 1970s, the USSR had acquired access to various facilities of military utility in Somalia, including the port of Berbera, and in 1974 it concluded a treaty of friendship and cooperation with the Somali government — the first such document it had signed with any African country. Nonetheless, the relationship quickly soured in the mid-1970s as Moscow attempted to cultivate links as well with the revolutionary military government that had replaced Haile Selassie in Ethiopia in 1974. Ultimately, Soviet wooing of the rulers in Addis Ababa led Siad Barre not only to expel all Soviet advisers but also to deny the USSR access to any military facilities in Somalia. Moscow responded by moving to bolster its relations with Ethiopia. As mentioned previously, it conducted a massive air- and sealift of weapons, Cuban combat troops, and Soviet military advisers into the country to repel the invading Somali forces that sought to wrest the Ogaden from Addis Ababa's control. This effort resulted in an investment of nearly $2 billion in arms alone.[111]

As of the early 1980s, the Soviet position in the Horn rests basically on the USSR's tie with Mengistu Haile-Mariam and the Provisional Military Government of Socialist Ethiopia (PMGSE). This situation probably causes a fair amount of discomfort in Moscow, for a good deal of friction has developed in the Soviet-Ethiopian relationship.

The friction has a variety of roots.[112] Soviet officials have pressed Mengistu to set up a vanguard party to institutionalize the Ethiopian revolution, but Mengistu has moved at a highly deliberate pace in this regard. He announced the formation of a Commission for Organizing the Party of the Working People of Ethiopia (COPWE) in December 1979, but even though this body held its second congress in January 1983, the constituent gathering for a full-fledged vanguard party will not take place before September 1984, when COPWE is supposed to meet for its third congress. This schedule reflects the present weakness of COPWE's structure around the country. Equally critical from Moscow's standpoint, COPWE functions as essentially an instrument of the PMGSE, rather than vice versa.

Although the USSR has supplied more than $2 billion in arms to the Addis Ababa government, it has not provided funds to pay for the greatly expanded military establishment of Ethiopia. In fact, even the local expenses of the estimated 13 thousand Cuban troops that remain in Ethiopia in the wake of the Ogaden war of 1977–1978 must be met from the Ethiopian budget. No less telling, the $2 billion in weapons and equipment that Moscow furnished did not come gratis, and Soviet officials apparently have taken to reminding their counterparts in Addis Ababa of this unpaid debt. (Whether Moscow will ever actually try to call in the debt, as opposed to using it for political leverage, is perhaps an open question.)

The military equipment that the USSR provided to Ethiopia also has sometimes proved less than durable. To compound the problem, Soviet officials insist that major repair work on heavy military and technical equipment that Ethiopia has purchased must be done in the USSR, and they have asked the Ethiopians to pay the transportation costs involved.

In view of the heavy military burden and the dwindling of Western economic aid to about $190 million a year in the early 1980s, the PMGSE has tried to persuade Moscow to give greater economic assistance to Ethiopia, in the form of grants and low-interest loans, but the results have not satisfied the Ethiopians. During 1980–1981, the USSR extended a mere $10 million in additional credits to the Addis Ababa government. Moscow is said to have doubts about Ethiopia's capacity to absorb more aid efficiently. Particularly galling to Addis Ababa has been the refusal of the USSR to agree to furnish oil imports at preferential prices on a long-term basis, for in recent years 70 percent or more of Ethiopia's foreign exchange earnings have been going to pay for petroleum imports. There have been rumors of late, however, that in 1982 Moscow at least consented to deliver oil to Ethiopia at preferential prices on short-term credit.

Finally, the presence of Soviet advisers with the Ethiopian military and East German advisers with the Ethiopian intelligence service has not helped Mengistu crush the Eritrean rebellion. Although both the USSR and Cuba have pushed for reconciliation between Addis Ababa and the Eritrean rebels, Mengistu has proved unwilling to make any concessions that might bring about such a development, and the Eritreans have adopted an equally intransigent posture. In this context, Moscow, in contrast with Havana, has deemed that it must aid Mengistu in his battle with the rebels, at least until the Eritreans show a desire to come to the bargaining table. Mengistu, however, has not gained what he had hoped from this assistance. In fact, the offensive that the Ethiopian army mounted with the help of Soviet military advisers and East German intelligence advisers in the latter part of 1982 ended in a stalemate. Worse yet, it yielded considerable loss of life and demoralization among Ethiopian troops. As a consequence, Mengistu has now replaced many of the East German technical advisers in his intelligence service with Israelis, thereby reviving a relationship that had existed in the mid-1970s before Ethiopia became heavily involved with the USSR. He has also installed Israelis as advisers to his own bodyguard.

Thus far in the 1980s, Soviet-Ethiopian frictions have not seriously jeopardized the Soviet position in Ethiopia, but Moscow, mindful of the volatility that has characterized its past relations with the Horn, may well feel uneasy about the long-range opportunities for the USSR in the African country. If so, Soviet leaders could want to take out some insurance that the USSR will continue to play a key role in the area in the years ahead. Somalia could conceivably offer the USSR new openings of this sort in the 1980s.

In light of overt Soviet backing of the political opposition to Siad Barre since 1982,[113] it is highly unlikely that Moscow could effect any sort of rapprochement with Somalia as long as he holds onto the reigns of power there, but his grip on authority has weakened in the 1980s. His problems stem from the country's economic malaise and the flood of refugees out of the Ogaden as well as from straightforwardly political factors.

To take economic considerations first, Somalia confronts some grim statistics. Long one of the poorest countries in the world, it managed to achieve an average annual growth rate of real GDP per capita of only 0.9 percent during 1970–1980. Even more debilitating, it recorded a negative average annual growth rate of total food production per capita from 1969–1971 to 1977–1979. As a consequence, it has to import half the food consumed within its borders. These imports, in combination with the increased price that Mogadishu must pay for the oil that it buys, have exhausted the state's reserves of foreign exchange.[114]

In part, the economic situation reflects factors over which Siad Barre's government has had little, if any, control. For example, the average annual growth rate of the population in 1970–1979 hit a high of 2.3 percent, and a severe drought in 1974–1975 wiped out the herds of almost a quarter of a million nomads. But a portion of the blame must be borne by Siad Barre's policies of "wealth-sharing based on knowledge" — his version of "scientific socialism." Strict state control of the economy resulted in low farm prices, and price controls in the city adversely affected the countryside's terms of trade with urban centers. Thus, there was a disincentive for the rural sector to produce.[115]

The economic problems have been exacerbated by the influx of more than a million refugees from Ethiopia in the wake of the fighting in the Ogaden in 1977–1978. More than 700 thousand of these came with nothing and exist in total dependence in some 40 camps spread across the country. A large share of Somalia's food imports go to keep them alive. For instance, two-thirds of the $90 million that the United States provided in food assistance to Mogadishu in 1980 wound up in their hands.[116]

Although drought in the areas from which the refugees fled contributed to their exodus, the main reason for it lay in fear of the Ethiopian hostility evoked by the invasion of the Ogaden by Siad Barre's government in 1977. The Somalis and other minority Ethiopian nationalities near the territory of Somalia found themselves viewed as actual or potential traitors and treated accordingly. In this sense, then, Siad Barre has to accept a share of responsibility for bringing about the deluge of refugees.

Whatever the degree to which Siad Barre may have caused these difficulties, they have sparked dissatisfaction with his government. This, in turn, has fed political discontent, which has been growing on other grounds as well. First, there is the resentment of northerners (from former British Somaliland), and particularly the Majerteen tribal confederation, concerning the domination of the government by southerners (from former Italian Somaliland) — notably, members of the Marrehaan tribal group. Many northerners feel that they should have their own separate state or at least autonomy within Somalia. Second, Siad Barre's handling of the 1977–1978 war with Ethiopia has come in for substantial criticism. Some believe that he did not pursue the undertaking aggressively enough; others blame him for losing the conflict. Third, Siad Barre's tilt toward the United States in recent years, and especially his offer to Washington of access to facilities such as the port of Berbera during military crises, has aroused opposition. This has been intensified by what is perceived in some Somali quarters as the relatively low payoff for Somalia from Siad Barre's cooperation with the United States. U.S. military aid to Somalia, for instance, totaled only $15 million in fiscal 1982, and it is expected to run to $15 million again in fiscal 1983. Even the proposed figure for fiscal 1984 is just $40 million.[117]

This political unrest has manifested itself overtly in several ways. During the late 1970s organized opposition to Siad Barre's rule began to take shape, and by the early 1980s it had reached significant proportions. Active groups included the Somali National Movement (SNM), the Somali Salvation Front, the Somali Workers Party, and the Democratic Front for the Liberation of Somalia. The first, composed largely of northerners of the Majerteen, maintained headquarters in London but used Djibouti as a base for staying in touch with Somalia's internal scene. The second, dominated by northerners too, had operational headquarters in Ethiopia. The last functioned out of Aden and may have received indirect Soviet aid. In October 1981, the Somali Salvation Front, the Somali Workers Party, and the Democratic Front for the Liberation of Somalia joined together to establish the Democratic Front for the Salvation of Somalia (DFSS). Although the SNM did not enter the new Front, it did conclude an agreement of cooperation with the Front. Both groups pledged to conduct armed struggle against Siad Barre's government.

In January 1982, DFSS forces managed to seize a border town in the north and hold it for a day or so. Subsequently, the DFSS even induced the Addis Ababa government to commit regular Ethiopian troops to help it capture some Somalian territory, apparently in the hope of sparking a general uprising against Siad Barre. This venture got under way in July 1982, but although it succeeded in establishing two salients in central Somalia, it failed to achieve any broader purposes. In fact, the Ethiopian involvement wound up being counterproductive, for it permitted Siad Barre to appeal to Somali nationalism and even to obtain emergency military aid from the United States. The SNM has also lived up to its promise to carry out military activities against Siad Barre. In January 1983, for instance, it staged a raid on Mardera central prison and freed 724 prisoners. This incident prompted the Somali president to close the border with Djibouti and to impose martial law in Hargeisa, the regional capital of the north.[118]

The guerrilla movements seeking to free the Ogaden from Ethiopian control have split over the question of relations with Siad Barre's government. In fact, the Western Somali Liberation Front in late January and early February 1981 ousted its entire 70-man Central Committee on the issue. The new 50-man Central Committee sought to distance itself from Mogadishu.[119]

Finally, the army, the chief pillar of Siad Barre's power, has suffered a growing number of mutinies and defections. Not long after Somalia's defeat in the Ogaden in 1978, a group of officers, mostly from the north, attempted unsuccessfully to topple Siad Barre. Then a period of relative harmony ensued for several years. In January 1982, however, there was trouble in the Somali Eighth Army, which is stationed in the northern part of the country. Garrisons in Hargeisa and nearby areas rose against the government after it executed 11 local officials for permitting DFSS forces to take over a border town briefly. April witnessed the desertion of General Adde Musa Hirsi to the DFSS, and June brought announcement of the uncovering of a conspiracy to oust Siad Barre by his third vice president, Brigadier General Ismail Ali Abokar, and several present and former cabinet members. During the push of Ethiopian-DFSS forces into central Somalia in the summer of 1982, there were even well-documented surrenders of Somali units without the slightest struggle.[120]

Siad Barre's response to such open dissent has if anything tended to complicate his problems. He has resorted liberally to force and even to the firing squad to silence his opponents. Although in the spring of 1982 he did lift the martial law that he had imposed in October 1980, he reinstituted it at least temporarily in the north in January 1983 after the SNM raid on Mardera central prison. Perhaps more damaging, he has edged the vast majority of civilians out of key jobs in the government administration and ruling party — thereby returning to heavy reliance upon the military to sustain his authority — and he has handed out new responsibilities based largely upon loyalty to him personally rather than upon competence.[121]

In sum, it is well within the realm of possibility that Siad Barre's rule will not last through the 1980s. If he falls, his successor(s) might prove more receptive to Soviet overtures than he has been since the late 1970s. This would almost certainly be the case if the DFSS assumed the dominant role in the country, for its program calls not only for denying the United States military access to the facilities at Berbera but also for reestablishing diplomatic, trade, and cultural relations with Ethiopia, Cuba, and "other socialist nations."[122] The likelihood would not be as overwhelming if the more moderate SNM or some currently serving member(s) of the officer corps came to power, but it would still be high.

Zaire

Zaire boasts a number of assets that render it of consequence. It covers the second largest area of any country in sub-Saharan Africa, and it has a bigger population than all but three other states in the region. It is situated at the strategic heart of the African continent, with no fewer than nine other countries bordering upon it. Its vast resources give it considerable economic potential. Indeed, it has already become a major exporter of minerals; its supplies of cobalt are of particular importance to the industrialized countries of the world.

The USSR has demonstrated an awareness of these attributes for more than two decades. As noted earlier, Moscow, soon after Zaire won its independence from Belgium in 1960, developed a fairly close relationship with Patrice Lumumba, the new state's first premier. It even agreed to supply aircraft and trucks to help him restore his central government's authority over the breakaway province of Katanga (now Shaba). Lumumba's ouster in September 1960 and subsequent death in early 1961 destroyed this initial Soviet foothold, but over the ensuing years Moscow has repeatedly tried to reassert its influence in the country. It has done so, however, largely by assisting various forces challenging the central government. These have included the Lumumbist regime headed by Antoine Gizenga and headquartered in Stanleyville in 1960–1961; the insurrectionary movement that developed in the northern and eastern provinces of the country in 1964–1965 under the leadership of men like Christophe Gbenye and Gaston-Emile Soumialot; and the National Front for the Liberation of the Congo (FNLC) that staged invasions of Shaba from Angolan bases in 1977 and 1978.[123]

To date, such activities have netted the USSR little, and although Moscow's relations with the Kinshasa government have improved since the late 1970s, they can only be described as correct, not warm. Yet this overall state of affairs could well alter before the close of the 1980s.

Although Mobutu Sese Seko has ruled Zaire since 1965, his government is now widely conceded to be among the shakiest in sub-Saharan Africa. Its instability arises from a wide array of factors.

For any Zairian government, regionalism would constitute a major problem, for the country has no tradition of strong central authority. Prior to its consolidation under Belgian auspices, the territory that now makes up the state of Zaire was under the control of more than 200 different tribes. Moreover, Belgium imposed a rather rudimentary and highly decentralized administrative structure on the country during the period of its colonial rule, from 1908 to 1960. It is hardly surprising, therefore, that Zaire nearly fragmented after the Belgians granted it independence. Only the military intervention of, first, the United Nations and, later, the Western powers enabled the Leopoldville (now Kinshasa) government to keep the country intact in the early and mid-1960s. Even then, particularism remained at high pitch. Over ensuing years, broader regional identifications have become more salient than tribal ones, with the rapid diffusion of the major linguae francae, especially Lingala and Swahili. However, there continues to be at best a weak sense of Zairian "nationhood."[124]

To a considerable extent, Mobutu has accentuated the difficulties that confront him in this regard, even though he has laid great stress on combatting ethnicity. To maintain his own dominance, he has followed a policy of divide and conquer, by pitting one region against another. Perhaps more crucial, he has drawn the key members of his own entourage, and especially his security forces, from his native Equateur Province. This predominance of Equateurians serves to arouse animosity toward his government on the part of persons from other regions.[125]

Under Mobutu, there has been an impoverishment of the masses of the population. Across the 1970–1980 period, Zaire's real GDP per capita declined at an average annual rate of 2.6 percent. As a result, the country's GNP per capita stood at less than $200 in 1981. Even this figure, however, presents a highly misleading picture of the lot of the typical

Zairian in the early 1980s. The politically privileged, especially members of what is known as the "presidential family," have amassed considerable wealth. Estimates of the fortune of Mobutu himself vary but consistently run into the millions of dollars. Rampant inflation has also greatly reduced the real value of the income of the average Zairian. During 1960–1970, inflation averaged 29.9 percent a year; during 1970–1979, the figure climbed to 31.4 percent. Thus, although the median income for a Zairian working in private industry in 1980 was 170 zaires a month, this amounted to less than half the cost of feeding the typical Zairian family of six. To make matters worse, the general availability of food has decreased, despite a rise in food imports from virtually no kilograms per capita in 1975 to 2.9 kilograms per capita in 1979. This reflects a negative growth rate in the state's total food production per capita between 1969–1971 and 1977–1979 averaging 1.4 percent a year.[126]

Responsibility for this general trend cannot be fixed wholly upon the Mobutu government. The rate of growth of Zaire's population, for example, took a big jump in the 1970s. Whereas the population had increased by an average of 2.0 percent a year in 1960–1970, the figure for 1970–1979 was 2.7 percent.[127] The price of copper, the state's chief export item, also plummeted from about $1.50 a pound to $0.50–0.60 a pound in the mid-1970s. As a consequence, Zaire's copper revenues fell to roughly half what they had been in the early 1970s. At the same time, the worldwide rise in oil prices caused its import bill for petroleum and petroleum products to mount sharply. Although the price of cobalt, Zaire's other key mineral export, soared from about $5.50 to $25 a pound in the late 1970s, this development by no means offset the increase in the cost of petroleum imports. Moreover, the price of cobalt had dropped back to $17 a pound by the early 1980s.[128]

Nonetheless, the government, with a substantial record of economic mismanagement, has played a major role in bringing about Zaire's economic decline. During the early 1970s, for instance, it engaged in extravagant borrowing abroad to finance a grandiose development program, many of whose projects had doubtful prospects from the outset. As a result, Zaire by the beginning of the 1980s had a debt to the International Monetary Fund and Western banks that exceeded $4 billion. Service liabilities alone on this debt amounted to 34.0 percent of export earnings in 1978 and 30.1 percent of such earnings in 1979. These liabilities left the country with enormous balance-of-payments deficits that it was unable to handle without rescheduling its debt payments. Furthermore, debt service has remained a problem ever since, and annual revisions of the repayment schedule have proved necessary to keep the country from going bankrupt.[129] On the domestic front, the government's budget deficit leaped from 310 million zaires in 1977 to 573 million zaires in 1978 and then dropped only slightly, to 558 million zaires, in 1979. During this three-year period, however, the country's GDP in real terms was declining. Particularly telling was the explanation for the jump in the deficit. Government receipts increased substantially, from 699 million zaires in 1977 to 1,979 million zaires in 1979, but the rate of expansion of expenditures outstripped that of revenues. Expenditures rose from 1,008 million zaires in 1977 to 2,537 million zaires in 1979. A similar pattern has prevailed in the 1980s, with excessive government spending producing large budget deficits. Because of a drop in receipts from the state mining corporation (Gecamines), the size of the deficits has even grown. In 1982, the shortfall reached nearly 3 billion zaires.[130]

In addition, Mobutu, even though he has railed publicly against official corruption, has created an environment in which it flourishes. As noted earlier, he and his entourage have accumulated sizable fortunes from their political positions, and their actions have spoken louder than Mobutu's words to public sector employees. Moreover, the failure of Mobutu's government to put a rein on inflation during the 1970s has by all accounts transformed graft from a widespread phenomenon to an utterly pervasive one. The sharp escalation of inflation caused a rapid erosion of the value of the nominal wages of public sector employees, and officials sought to take advantage of their jobs to compensate for their losses.[131]

More important, growing, if indeterminate, numbers of Zairians have evinced an inclination to blame Mobutu and his system for their plight. Thus far, this disposition does not appear to have manifested itself in much organized opposition within the country, but there has been plenty of evidence of such an attitude in private conversations among Zairians and between Zairians and Westerners in recent years.[132]

Mobutu's style of rule has also alienated many people, especially among the young and in the expanding ranks of the educated elite. He founded and heads the Popular Movement of the Revolution (MPR), a political superstructure deemed to embrace every member of the population from birth, and he has crushed all political groupings outside that official framework. Moreover, to ensure that no new ones take shape – at least inside the country – he has developed a wide network of informers. Although he did create a legislative National Assembly and hold competitive elections for it under the banner of his ruling party in 1977, he never regarded it as a limitation on his exercise of power. Indeed, when members of the assembly later publicly criticized him, his advisers, and his family for corruption, he consigned it to political limbo. Its functions have now essentially been assumed by the newly created Central Committee of the MPR – whose members are appointed by Mobutu. Mobutu has also indulged in blatant nepotism. He has given many of his relatives top state jobs or bestowed official patronage on their private undertakings. Last but not least, he has carried out repeated purges and constant rotation of personnel at the upper reaches of the state apparatus. In this manner, he has sought to foster high levels of insecurity and prevent any conceivable rival from developing a power base.[133]

Finally, the armed forces, the key prop of Mobutu's rule, have glaring weaknesses as a military force, and they could prove unequal to the task of defending the government if Mobutu faced a serious armed challenge. When irregulars of the Angola-based FNLC moved into Shaba in 1977 and again in 1978, the Zairian army, although superior in numbers to the raiders, could not handle the situations without outside help. In the latter case, Mobutu even had to call in troops from the Western powers to repel the attackers. Since 1978, it is true, the Zairian armed forces have received additional training and equipment from such sources as Belgium, France, the United States, and China. Yet their effectiveness in combat is subject to doubt. Mobutu indirectly conceded their deficiencies in January 1983 by signing a five-year military cooperation agreement with Israel. Under the terms of this agreement, Israeli advisers are to assist with restructuring the 12 thousand-man Kamanyola Division in Shaba and to train Zairian naval units at Kalemnie, on the bank of Lake Tanganyika, and a new artillery battalion in Hbanza-Ngungu, southwest of Kinshasa. Whether Mobutu will allow the Israelis to turn the armed forces into a professional organization, however, remains open to question, for such an organization could present a threat to his authority.[134]

Should the Mobutu era in Zaire end during the 1980s, there seems little chance that a militant radical regime even of the Angolan or Mozambican types would emerge there.[135] Either of two more likely outcomes, however, would create new openings for the USSR. First, the Zairians might have difficulties putting together a central government, and civil war along regional and ethnic lines could result. Because individual contestants would probably seek support from outside quarters, Moscow would no doubt have an opportunity to back some elements in the conflict. Its patronage might seem particularly attractive if Cuban troops were still in Angola and Soviet leaders could call upon them for military operations on the ground. Second, Mobutu might be succeeded by a nationalistic government bent on pursuing the sort of policies that he himself attempted to follow in his "Zairization" phase in the early 1970s. In keeping with such an orientation, the new government might wish to strike a less pro-Western, more nonaligned stance than Mobutu has assumed in recent years. One aspect of this kind of posture would be closer relations with Moscow.

Southern Africa

Multiple considerations give Southern Africa a high degree of inherent importance. The area contains both the wealthiest state and the third largest one with respect to population in the whole of sub-Saharan Africa—namely, South Africa. The sea lanes around the coast of Southern Africa constitute a major transit route between the Indian Ocean and the Atlantic Ocean for both commercial and military vessels. As already discussed, the substantial dependence of the Western powers on Persian Gulf oil in recent years has heightened the significance of this transit route considerably; as of the early 1980s the bulk of the oil destined for Western Europe and about 20 percent of that going to the United States travel along it. Last but by no means least, the region, as also mentioned earlier, is a treasure trove of minerals. Indeed, it represents the only major source aside from the USSR of four minerals – platinum, chromium, vanadium, and manganese – of great consequence to advanced industrial societies. Soviet analysts have long called attention to these features of Southern Africa, and during the 1960s and early 1970s the USSR managed to winnow its way into the affairs of the region in small ways. It emerged as a champion of the ANC of South Africa. It also forged links with the MPLA of Angola, FRELIMO of Mozambique, ZAPU of Zimbabwe, and SWAPO of Namibia, and it provided them with some assistance in their struggles against white-minority rule. It even established diplomatic ties with Zambia in the wake of that country's acquisition of independence in 1964.

But it was not until after the military coup in Lisbon in April 1974 and Portugal's subsequent decision to dissolve its African empire that the USSR truly focused on the area. Then it sought to make up for lost time. Although, as pointed out previously, Moscow rejected the claims of the ruling parties of Angola and Mozambique to be "genuine" Marxist-Leninist entities, it nevertheless fashioned close ties with the governments of the two countries. Indeed, it signed treaties of friendship and cooperation with them and functioned as their chief arms supplier. It became the main source of arms as well for Zambia and for Namibia's SWAPO, and at least until the last phases of the guerrilla struggle in Zimbabwe, it served in a similar capacity for ZAPU.[136] It even set up diplomatic relations with Botswana and Lesotho, two of the least ideological states in the area.

The triumph of Robert Mugabe in the March 1980 elections that ended the strife in Zimbabwe, to be sure, halted the steady expansion of the Soviet role in Southern Africa. Because Moscow had long favored Joshua Nkomo's ZAPU over Mugabe's ZANU and had channeled most of its concrete aid to ZAPU during the guerrilla war against the white-dominated government of Ian Smith, Mugabe displayed a distinct reserve toward the USSR. Although his new government moved quickly to enter into official relations with China, the Soviet Union's arch Communist rival, it waited until February 1981 to give the USSR permission to set up an embassy in Salisbury. Even then, it required Soviet officials to agree formally to maintain no political ties in Zimbabwe outside official channels.[137]

Yet this reversal could wind up being merely a temporary setback for Moscow. Much will depend upon the course of developments with respect to Namibia and South Africa. Here one needs to distinguish between the two situations.

As for Namibia, there is a chance that the USSR could find itself deprived of significant new opportunities there by the negotiations going on with the assistance of a Western contact group operating under the auspices of the United Nations. Indeed, Moscow could even discover that some of the openings that the guerrilla war in Namibia has afforded it in Angola in recent years could at least diminish.

Since 1982, it is true, the negotiations on the fate of Namibia have bogged down over the issue of the Cuban troops in Angola. South Africa has insisted that any settlement in Namibia must be linked to the withdrawal of Cuban troops, while Angola has hesitated to commit itself to ask the Cubans to leave as long as South African military forces remain in Namibia and continue to aid UNITA. But it is not inconceivable that the Western contact powers could find a way to surmount this problem.

If so, most questions regarding a constitution for an independent Namibia have already been resolved, and the major stumbling blocs left regarding the details of a settlement concern the mechanics of the elections. Were these obstacles eliminated, however, a final hurdle would remain. Virtually all obervers at present believe that SWAPO would win freely contested elections and dominate any government that emerged from them. Whether South Africa could tolerate such an outcome continues to be uncertain. The split in the ruling Nationalist Party of South Africa that occurred in early 1982 might eventually facilitate adoption of such a position by the South African government, yet the immediate impact of the split has been to make the government tread lightly on the Namibian issue. In fact, South African armed forces have launched repeated raids into Angola since 1980 with the apparent aim of destroying SWAPO as a military entity. Furthermore, Pretoria has now resumed direct rule over Namibia, in the wake of the breakup of the local multiracial government under the Democratic Turnhalle Alliance in late 1982.

Overcoming such formidable difficulties will clearly not be an easy task, but it does not yet appear to fall into the realm of the impossible. If a peaceful, internationally acceptable settlement does take place, the USSR will have vastly less influence on any new government that assumes authority than it would if SWAPO achieved power by force of arms. Although a SWAPO-controlled government would probably want to establish some links with the USSR, it would not owe Moscow any great debts. A government under the domination of other forces would have even less reason to behave deferentially toward the USSR.

Resolution of the Namibian conflict would reduce the importance of the USSR to Angola, too, for Angola would not then be a primary base for insurrectionary activities directed at the Pretoria government. Under such circumstances, Angolan leaders might well desire to decrease not only the Cuban but also the Soviet presence in their country. Since early 1982, the USSR has seemed to be trying to forestall such an eventuality by laying solid foundations for long-term relations with Angola. In January 1982, as already mentioned, the two countries concluded an economic cooperation agreement covering the period to 1990. Soviet officials talked about extending $2 billion in credits to the Luanda government under terms of this accord, and they actually signed contracts later in 1982 for projects amounting to $400 million.

Despite all efforts, of course, the negotiations on Namibia's future could still collapse. If they do, the USSR's opportunities in Southern Africa will almost certainly enlarge substantially. The black African states will probably push for the imposition of economic sanctions against South Africa and for a step-up in the guerrilla warfare in Namibia. As these states are well aware, the Soviet Union is the only great power in a position and conceivably disposed to help in both endeavors, particularly the latter.

With respect to South Africa, the outlook is less ambiguous from Moscow's standpoint. To begin with, strife between blacks and whites within South Africa appears likely to grow worse before it gets better. During recent years, the ruling whites have taken a variety of steps to try to ease tensions in South African society. These have included proposals to give some political rights to coloreds and Indians, acceptance of the inevitability of a permanent black urban population, trade union rights for black workers, promise of free primary and secondary education for all black children, and relaxation of the color bar in industry. Yet such moves have failed to address the fundamental issue – political rights for the black majority. Indeed, the government has time and again denied any intention of tackling this matter. Hand in hand with the concessions, moreover, has gone increased repression of black political activity. Thus, blacks – and especially the mounting numbers of militants among younger blacks – have tended to see these concessions as merely cosmetic in nature.

It is not inconceivable, of course, that there might be a quickening of the pace of change in the years ahead. The Nationalist split in early 1982 sheared off the right wing of the party and could mark the beginning of a broad realignment of South African politics. In such a realignment, the Nationalist Party would emerge as a centrist body (in South African terms), attracting moderate Afrikaners and English-speakers to its ranks and perhaps even forging alliances with parties representing coloreds and Indians if these social groups actually receive the franchise. Such a process would obviously make the dismantling of the apartheid structure much easier.

Whether the pace of change picks up or not, however, modifications in the internal status quo probably will not take place at a speed that will satisfy at least significant portions of the black community. Under such circumstances, there is likely to be a desire to accelerate them. This could manifest itself not only in heightened domestic violence but also in greater efforts to bring pressure to bear on the South African government from outside the country. Undertakings of the latter sort might cause blacks to look with increased favor on the USSR.

The precise degree to which South African blacks will seek help from Moscow will probably depend in large measure on how black politics within the country evolve. Moscow's links with South African blacks have traditionally been through Soviet ties with the outlawed ANC. Although the original champion of black political rights in South Africa, this organization now has a multiracial character. In fact, whites who are members of the South African Communist Party not only belong to it but even seem to exercise substantial influence within it. In recent years, however, a variety of other black forces have emerged within South Africa that adhere to a posture of black nationalism; moreover, many of these have managed to function overtly there. The USSR has carefully refrained from attacking at least most of these groups, and in the fall of 1982 it even entered into direct contacts with Gatsha Buthelezi, chief minister of the black homeland of KwaZulu and head of the Zulu-based Inkatha, while he was visiting the United States.[138] Yet Moscow remains identified essentially with the ANC and will in all likelihood find it hard to alter this state of affairs. If the ANC's multiracial approach and the role of white South African Communists in the organization become sources of a sharpening of political divisions within the black community, such an identification could prove disadvantageous to the USSR. But if blacks decide to form a united front both among themselves and with supporters of black political rights from other racial elements within South Africa, the ANC affords a logical body for this purpose, and long-time association with it could prove highly beneficial to the USSR.

In the absence of rapid and massive improvements in the lot of blacks within South Africa, conflict between South Africa and its neighbors seems destined to escalate during the 1980s. Although the black African states in Southern Africa have recognized the Afrikaners as a "white African tribe" because of their long-term presence on the continent, most of these states continue to be committed to an early demise of the apartheid system in South Africa and the emergence of a black-run government there. Hence, they will probably at minimum lend clandestine support to black South Africans seeking to bring down the Afrikaner government. The South African government, for its part, has evinced a growing inclination to use economic and military pressure to force South Africa's black-controlled neighbors to cease what it considers to be blatant interference in internal South African affairs. For instance, it attempted to exert economic leverage on Zimbabwe's policies by first giving notice in 1981 of an intention to cancel the preferential trade agreement between Zimbabwe and South Africa and then extending the agreement in 1982. Similarly, it launched raids into Matola, Mozambique, in early 1981 and Maseru, Lesotho, in late 1982 to knock out the facilities of the ANC there.

In this regard, it is crucial to remember that South Africa dominates the region economically and militarily. From an economic standpoint, South Africa qualifies as a real powerhouse. As late as 1978, it accounted for about 20 percent of all Africa's production of goods and services and nearly 80 percent of that of Southern Africa alone. That same year, it boasted 86 percent of the whole continent's steel output, more than 50 percent of its electric power production, 60 percent of its rail traffic, 43 percent of its registered motor vehicles, 42 percent of its telephones, and 40 percent of its industrial output. The country was also the only major food exporter in Africa.[139]

Perhaps more to the point, the rest of Southern Africa is highly dependent upon South Africa in an economic sense. Although no precise breakdowns for individual states are available, all the black African countries of the region except Angola get most of their food imports – particularly maize, wheat, processed foods, and meat – from South Africa. In some cases, such as Botswana, Lesotho, Swaziland, and Zimbabwe, the same is true with respect to oil. South Africa's immediate neighbors also rely heavily upon South Africa for different kinds of machinery and spare parts; furthermore, many of them derive a lot of their export income from sales to it. Most of the states in the region provide migrant workers to South African enterprises. Some of the key transportation routes of countries adjacent to South Africa pass through the Republic, and in certain instances (for example, Botswana and Lesotho) the only access that the states have to world markets lies through South African ports. Finally, South African capital finances development projects in a few countries in the region. In 1980, the total figure for these reached nearly $200 million.[140]

On the military front, South Africa's capabilities greatly outweigh those of the rest of the region's states together. As of July 1982, the Republic had standing armed forces of 81,400, and it could mobilize 404,500 men on short notice. In contrast, the other countries in Southern Africa could muster only about 123 thousand men. A prolonged call-up by Pretoria, to be sure, would greatly disrupt the national economy, but the availability of such a force on even a short-term basis still has a profound psychological impact. In the critical realm of combat aircraft, South Africa enjoyed an overwhelming advantage. It possessed more than 400 combat planes in both operational and training units, while the total for the other countries in the region amounted to only about half that figure. Moreover, the South African inventory included 48 French Mirage III and 45 F-1 fighter aircraft — both more advanced planes than any of which a black state in the area could boast. The one domain in which the black African countries as a whole appeared to enjoy superiority was tanks. They had nearly 650, as compared with some 250 for South Africa. However, it is important to keep in mind here that mobilization of more than 375 for an attack from a single direction would present enormous logistical problems, for the tanks of the black African countries are divided among Angola, Mozambique, Zambia, and Zimbabwe. As far as naval combatants were concerned, South Africa possessed 20 and had an additional 6 on order, while the other states in Southern Africa could claim just 9. Although Pretoria denies that it has developed nuclear weapons, there can be no doubt that it enjoys the resources and technical know-how to do so. The same does not apply to any other country in the region. Last but not least, South Africa boasts an industrialized economy that has produced roughly half of the weapons and equipment in the hands of its armed forces at the moment. No other Southern African state comes close to such a degree of military independence.[141]

If South Africa continues to employ pressure tactics in its relations with the black-ruled countries in Southern Africa — and there is every reason to suppose that it will — these states will probably seek to offset their vulnerabilities vis-à-vis Pretoria. In fact, they have already begun to do so. For example, all of them participated in the formation of the

Southern African Development Cooperation Conference (SADCC) in April 1980. A long-range goal of this organization is to reduce the dependence of the region's economies on South Africa.[142] Individual countries have also sought to beef up their capacities to resist South African military incursions. Zambia's acquisition of some sophisticated fighter aircraft in the early 1980s affords a good illustration.[143]

The accomplishment of both of these ends will require considerable input from outside the continent. Thus, the black states of Southern Africa might well turn increasingly to the USSR for support in the 1980s, especially in the military realm.

5

Constraints on Soviet Activities

If the sorts of opportunities for the USSR that have been outlined here actually materialize during the 1980s, Moscow must reach a number of decisions regarding them. Which of these openings should it attempt to exploit? How intensively should it seek to capitalize upon any of them, and what resources should it commit to such endeavors?

In making decisions on these matters, Soviet leaders will have to take into account several constraints that confront the USSR at present and are likely to continue to do so throughout the rest of the decade. Of these, three stand out as the most critical: the geopolitical priority that Moscow attaches to sub-Saharan Africa, the condition of the Soviet economy, and the USSR's military capabilities to operate in sub-Saharan Africa. Each deserves some discussion.

Geopolitical Priority

Sub-Saharan Africa currently falls well down on Moscow's list of geopolitical priorities. Since the Bolshevik Revolution of 1917, Europe has claimed the top spot in Soviet geopolitical concerns. It was from Europe that the main threats to the Soviet state originated during the interwar period, culminating in the traumatic German invasion of 1941. Moreover, Europe has constituted the primary arena of the USSR's competition with the United States since the end of World War II. The possibility that in the 1980s NATO may deploy intermediate-range missiles in Western Europe that could hit Soviet territory has now served to reinforce Europe's key importance in Moscow's eyes.

East Asia has ranked second in Soviet geopolitical thinking since the 1930s and 1940s, when the USSR from time to time engaged in armed combat with an expansionist Japan. The war on the Korean peninsula in the 1950s, which brought about U.S. intervention under UN auspices, confirmed for Soviet leaders the area's continuing significance to the USSR in the post-World War II era. However, it was the Sino-Soviet split in the early 1960s that demonstrated to Moscow how vital its stakes in the region are. In the mid-1960s, Mao Zedong's revival of Chinese complaints about the "unequal treaties" whereby Tsarist Russia had gained vast Asian territories from the Chinese Empire—in combination with Beijing's acquisition of nuclear weapons—convinced Soviet leaders that a potentially serious security threat existed on their eastern borders. The Sino-American and Sino-Japanese rapprochements of the 1970s simply reinforced that judgment.

Since the mid-1960s third place on the Soviet list has gone to the southern rimlands of the USSR—that is, the countries forming a broad arc south of the Soviet Union, from the Indian subcontinent around to North Africa. Prior to that time, it should be underscored, Moscow had bestowed this ranking on varied groupings of states. During the early post-revolutionary period, for instance, it accorded the honor to the countries to the USSR's immediate south. Later, with Josef Stalin's rise to power and the advent of the world depression, it broadened the focus to the colonies of the West

European powers more generally – first with the aim of weakening these powers in the European context, but afterward with the goal of encouraging them to resist the pressures of Fascist Germany. In the initial post-World War II years, it limited the ranking essentially to the colonies and newly emerging states of South and Southeast Asia. As empires collapsed and more and more colonies acquired their independence, Nikita Khrushchev expanded the scope of concern once again – to include Asia as a whole, then Africa as well, and ultimately even Latin America. However, disappointment with the behavior of many of the states in these areas soon caused him to narrow the definition of the ranking to those states that he deemed had genuine revolutionary potential. Conviction that there was little possibility for Communist breakthroughs in the Third World in the foreseeable future led Khrushchev's successors to abandon his concept of the ranking in the mid-1960s and to replace it with a focus on the southern rimlands of the USSR. In contrast with the flux of earlier years, no new shifts in the nature of the ranking have now occurred for a substantial period of time.

Sub-Saharan Africa lies somewhere below these three regions on the Soviet ladder of geopolitical priorities. Its exact position has fluctuated since the mid-1960s, in accordance with how the opportunities that Moscow has perceived there have compared with those it has discerned elsewhere.

There is always the possibility, to be sure, that the 1980s could bring a revision of these priorities, but the chances of such a development seem poor at best. The occupants of the top three spots on the list have held their positions for nearly two decades now, and those in the first two have done so far longer than that. Furthermore, the ranking represents a logical ordering of concerns from the viewpoint of Soviet security considerations. Even an outside observer trying to assess the sources of potential threats to the USSR's national security in the foreseeable future from Moscow's perspective would probably arrive at just such a ranking.

If the USSR does in fact persist in assigning a relatively low priority to sub-Saharan Africa in the years ahead, the
ramifications will be substantial. Whatever openings Moscow
may believe exist there will count for less than the opportunities and dangers that it perceives in regions of greater
geopolitical importance to it. Therefore, the latter opportunities and dangers will lay primary claim to its attention and
resources. If these opportunities and dangers become numerous and/or highly consequential in nature, Moscow may have
little choice but to neglect sub-Saharan Africa to some extent. After all, Soviet officials do not possess an infinite
amount of time to handle issues, nor has the USSR yet attained a state of omnipotence.

Events of the early 1980s have, to a certain degree, already compelled Soviet leaders to face such a tradeoff. Major developments of interest to Moscow have taken place in
all three of the areas highest on the Soviet list of geopolitical concerns. Although the USSR invaded Afghanistan at
the end of 1979 to eliminate what Soviet leaders saw as instability on their southern border, it failed to accomplish that
goal, for it has encountered stiff resistance from local guerrilla forces operating under an Islamic banner. Currently,
more than 100 thousand Soviet troops remain tied down
there battling the insurgents. Poland also entered upon a
period of turmoil after August 1980 and the birth of the free
trade union Solidarity. Even though General Wojciech Jaru-
zelski eased Soviet worries by imposing martial law in
December 1981 and subsequently banning Solidarity, the political and economic problems of the East European country
have continued to preoccupy Soviet rulers. During the same
period, significant new openings for Soviet exploitation appeared in Western Europe. Some grew out of West European
differences with the United States over the merits of détente;
others stemmed from mounting opposition on the part of
some segments of the West European populaces to the planned
deployment of Pershing II and cruise missiles on West Eu-

ropean soil. Then in 1982 China for the first time in two decades showed signs of a real desire for at least a limited rapprochement with the USSR, and negotiations between the two have been going on intermittently since the fall of that year.

With such issues in these three regions absorbing it, Moscow has ignored or downplayed some opportunities that have presented themselves in sub-Saharan Africa. Those for greater economic and military involvement with Mozambique afford a good example.[144]

Prevailing trends in Europe, East Asia, and the southern rimlands of the USSR suggest that, if anything, the constraints on Soviet activity in sub-Saharan Africa could increase during the remainder of the 1980s. The difficulties in Poland reflect a more general crisis besetting Eastern Europe as a whole, and it is not inconceivable that turmoil could break out elsewhere in the coming years. Romania is perhaps the leading candidate for such disturbances. In Western Europe, overt tensions within the NATO alliance may decline once intermediate-range missiles have been deployed or a firm decision has been taken not to deploy them, but the differences in perspectives between Western Europe and the United States are not likely to fade so easily. On the contrary, they could even grow more pronounced, especially if the economic situation in Western Europe fails to improve. Thus, they will probably continue to provide attractive openings upon which the USSR might seek to capitalize. The conflict in Afghanistan likewise seems destined to drag on indefinitely, with Moscow unprepared to withdraw its troops without insuring the survival of the Babrak Karmal regime and unwilling to risk world wrath by making the massive commitment of troops and matériel required to crush the rebels. At the same time, circumstances in Iran and the Persian Gulf more broadly could offer major new possibilities for Soviet maneuver. For example, although Iran's Islamic fundamentalist regime has recently cracked down on the Tudeh, the local Communist Party, by arresting many of its senior leaders,[145] Ayatollah Ruhollah Khomeini will almost certainly not last out the decade, and how much political turbulance his death will cause remains to be seen. Finally, East Asia is changing in ways that may induce Moscow to pay particularly close heed to the region in the future. Not only is China seriously weighing a rapprochement with the USSR, but Japan appears to be moving toward acceptance of a larger military role in the area.

The Soviet Economy

In recent years, the USSR has experienced mounting problems with its economy. Since the end of the 1960s, the Soviet Union's overall economic growth rate has been declining, and the falloff has been quite sharp since 1976. The average annual rate of growth of GNP hit 5.2 percent during 1966-1970 and then fell to 3.7 percent during 1971-1975, 2.7 percent during 1976-1980, and an estimated 2.0 percent during 1981-1982. In per capita terms, the figures went from 4.2 percent to 2.7 percent, 1.8 percent, and an estimated 1.2 percent during the same periods.[146]

Equally disturbing from the Soviet standpoint, the rate of growth of productivity has dropped in a similar fashion. Labor productivity increased at an average yearly rate of 3.2 percent in 1966-1970, but the pace of advance dropped to 2.0 percent in 1970-1975, 1.3 percent in 1976-1980, and 0.9 percent in 1980-1981. The rate of growth of total factor productivity (output per combined input of manhours, capital, and land) was even more dismal. From 1.0 percent a year on the average in 1966-1970, it went to −0.5 percent in 1970-1975, −0.9 percent in 1976-1980, and −1.3 percent in 1980-1981. Even if one looks only at the key sector of industry, the picture has been much the same. The growth rate of industrial labor productivity rose from an average annual figure of 3.1 percent in 1966–1970 to 4.4 percent in 1970–1975, but then it fell to 1.8 percent in 1976–1980 and 1.3 percent in 1980–1981. As for total factor productivity in industry, it increased at an average yearly rate of 0.5 percent in 1966–1970 and 1.0 percent in 1970–1975. Subsequently, however, the figure dropped to −1.0 percent in 1976–1980 and −1.8 percent in 1980–1981.[147]

There are two schools of thought among Western analysts about the reasons for these trends. One school sees the trends as evidence of major systemic problems in the Soviet economy. This view stresses the depletion of mineral resources in the European regions of the USSR, a perceived ossification of the mechanism of central planning, and declining morale among both workers and managers. The other school attributes the trends to a considerable extent to factors of a potentially more temporary nature. It points, first, to agricultural shortfalls brought on in part by bad weather. These, in turn, caused shortages of raw materials, diversions of labor, tieups in the transportation system, and reductions in available consumer goods – and hence a decrease in incentives for workers. This school of thought also cites the recent development of major bottlenecks in the Soviet economy, particularly in transportation, that have affected a wide range of sectors, and it argues that the Soviet decision in the 1970s to reduce the rate of growth of investment to permit a continued rise of consumption inadvertently resulted in a lack of sufficient resources to break these bottlenecks when they occurred.[148]

Neither school, however, disputes the impact of the trends on the USSR's foreign economic relations. The declining growth rate of the GNP has sharply restricted the funds that the Soviet leadership has felt it could spare for economic assistance to the Third World. Although the size of the Soviet economy today is twice what it was in 1965, it remains only half that of the United States. Yet since 1965 Moscow has poured large amounts of money into a major military buildup, and it has sought to keep the USSR's domestic political lid on securely by meeting the rising expectations of the Soviet populace with respect to consumption.[149] Doing both of these things in an era of declining economic growth has not left the USSR a lot of resources to devote to economic aid even to its Communist allies, let alone other countries. Soviet economic credits extended to the Third World as a whole did rise from $3,805 million in 1955-1964 to $6,225 million in 1965-1974 and to $10,635 million in 1975-1981,[150] but the last figure still represented only a small fraction of the total financial flows into these areas from all sources.[151]

The situation with respect to productivity has greatly diminished the USSR's capabilities for trading with the Third World in general and with sub-Saharan Africa in particular. To try to cope with the productivity problem in the industrial sector, Soviet leaders have relied primarily on high technology imports. Thus, purchases of industrial machinery and equipment accounted for an annual average of 33.8 percent of all Soviet purchases from abroad in 1971-1975 and 37.7 percent in 1976-1980. Because of the low productivity in agriculture, Soviet output of items such as grain has failed to meet domestic demands, and Moscow has had to supplement local production with imports. As a consequence, food purchases from abroad on the average constituted 26.8 percent of the USSR's total purchases from abroad each year in 1971-1975 and 26.6 percent in 1976-1979. Attempts to improve productivity of agriculture through increased use of fertilizer also kept the share of chemicals and fertilizer in Soviet imports at an annual average of 8.9 percent in 1971-1975 and 8.4 percent in 1976-1979.

In light of these various considerations, the USSR has been unable to buy many of the kinds of goods that Third

World countries typically offer for sale. For example, Soviet purchases from abroad of items such as fuel, minerals, and other raw materials comprised on the average but 14.8 percent of all Soviet purchases from abroad each year in 1971–1975 and 14.1 percent in 1976–1980.[152] Hence, Moscow's imports from Third World states in toto amounted to an annual average of only about 10 percent of Soviet imports in 1971–1980.[153] As late as 1978–1979, the share for sub-Saharan Africa alone averaged 1.0 percent each year of the USSR's total purchases from abroad.[154]

Assessments of the long-range prospects with regard to the Soviet economy's growth rates of GNP and productivity differ. On the one hand, those who believe the recent accelerated downturn in these growth rates reflects critical problems of a systemic character foresee no significant changes in a positive direction. They feel that, if anything, the situation could get worse. On the other hand, those who interpret developments of the last few years as largely the outcome of exceptional circumstances take a more optimistic view. Although they concede that growth retardation constitutes a long-term trend of the Soviet economy, they maintain that the economy could perform better in the future than it has in the recent past. For it to do so, there would have to be a favorable turn in certain influences over which the USSR has no control, and Moscow would need to alter some of its policies. As an example of the former, the proponents of this position cite the weather during the Soviet crop growing season; as an illustration of the latter, they point to relatively low inputs of investment.[155]

Nevertheless, most analysts concur that the 1980s will be a difficult decade for the Soviet economy. Even those who see a possibility of improved growth rates in the future do not expect such a rise to come quickly or easily. Indeed, they hold that Soviet leaders will probably even have to confront some hard tradeoffs among investment, consumption, and defense in the years just ahead.[156]

In this sort of context, the chances for any major expansion of the USSR's interaction with sub-Saharan Africa in the economic realm appear slim. It is conceivable, of course, that Moscow could allocate to the region a larger share of the resources that it has available to devote to the Third World. In fact, such a shift actually seems to have occurred in the early 1980s in the sphere of economic aid. Although the pace at which the USSR extended credits to the Third World slowed in 1980–1981 in comparison with that in 1975–1979, sub-Saharan Africa received $435 million of the 1980–1981 total of $2,515 million, while in 1975–1979 it garnered just $335 million of the overall sum of $8,120 million.[157] But as long as there is no significant enlargement of the portion of the Soviet economic pie that Moscow feels it can channel toward the Third World in general, such increases can only be limited ones, and all signs indicate that this kind of basic modification of Soviet economic priorities is not in the cards for the remainder of the decade.

Military Capabilities

Although the USSR has substantially enhanced its capacity to conduct military activities in sub-Saharan Africa since the early 1960s, that capacity continues to be limited in important ways. The limitations are often overlooked in discourses on Soviet advances in the military sphere.

At the outset, it is essential to distinguish between supply of arms and training and actual involvement in fighting in sub-Saharan Africa, whether in a logistical and supporting role or in a combat role. Moscow clearly has the means to provide enough arms and training indefinitely to help sustain prolonged guerrilla struggles and/or meet the needs of independent states in sub-Saharan Africa. The USSR, after all, is today the biggest producer of conventional arms in the world. Moreover, Moscow has traditionally evinced reluctance simply to discard weaponry it regards as obsolescent.[158] Thus, it is in the second domain that the limitations on Soviet capabilities lie.

To grasp the extent of these limitations some sense of the USSR's present capabilities for projection of power into the region is required. As already noted, there has been a permanent Soviet naval presence in the Indian Ocean near the eastern portions of sub-Saharan Africa since 1969, and a Soviet naval patrol has operated in the eastern Atlantic off the West African coast since 1970. The USSR also has air- and sealift forces that can ferry Soviet and/or allied troops in strength to the area. By and large, the airlift elements, which include some 600 planes directly under the command of the air force plus 1,100 planes in the civil Aeroflot fleet, are top-flight, and Moscow has been improving them by replacing the An-12 with the An-22 and the Il-76. The Il-76 can lift twice the payload over five times the distance that the AN-12 can. Although the sealift elements are not as impressive as the airlift ones – especially from a qualitative standpoint – the Soviet leadership is attempting to remedy their weaknesses. Since 1978, for example, the USSR has been deploying a new class of amphibious ships, each of which carries four landing craft, and construction of roll-on/roll-off ships proceeds apace, with more than 20 of them in service by the early 1980s.

As for troops, Moscow has in recent years created several new airborne divisions, so divisions of this type now number eight, although one is tied down in Afghanistan at the moment and is unavailable for use elsewhere. In addition, Soviet leaders have some special duty brigades that they can employ to supplement these divisions. With respect to naval infantry, the USSR has only 12 thousand men altogether. They are divided into five naval infantry regiments—each with three infantry battalions and one tank battalion—dispersed among the USSR's four fleets. For air cover, Soviet airborne and naval infantry troops must depend almost wholly on land-based planes. The USSR does possess some Kiev-class aircraft carriers, but these can accommodate only vertical-takeoff planes. Moreover, just two have entered full service, although a third is on trial runs and a fourth is under construction. As far as land-based aircraft are concerned, Soviet long- and medium-range bombers of the Bear, Bison, and Backfire types (330 in toto) do have the range to reach targets throughout much of sub-Saharan Africa without access to local facilities for refueling, but no other Soviet planes do. Indeed, most require two or more stops even to get to the region.[159]

These capabilities, while significant, fall well short of permitting the USSR to do whatever it chooses militarily in the region. That fact is perhaps best demonstrated by looking at them in terms of three prototypical situations in which Moscow might conceivably consider employing them in sub-Saharan Africa.

The first possible use might be against a black African state. From the standpoint of sheer numbers, the only black-ruled countries in the area that could currently mount a strong defense on even their own soil if Moscow decided to commit all its airborne divisions to an intervention are Ethiopia (with 250,500 men under arms), Nigeria (with 138 thousand men), and Somalia (with 62,550 men), and the forces of these three countries—particularly Somalia—would probably find coping with the better trained, better equipped Soviet forces an impossible job. The same conclusions would hold if Cuba intervened with the estimated 50 thousand troops that it could deploy abroad—at least as long as Havana could count on logistical backup from the USSR.[160] Furthermore, none of the black African states could sustain a conflict for long against either the USSR or a Soviet-Cuban alliance without outside help, for these states lack any real capacity for producing arms locally.[161]

In many places, however, the indigenous African military forces might refuse to fight on Soviet or Cuban terms. At least a substantial contingent of them might retreat to the countryside and carry on guerrilla warfare against the intervening Soviet or Cuban troops. Such opposition could confront the USSR or a Soviet-Cuban alliance with major problems because its forces would have poor knowledge of the turf and extended supply lines. Soviet experiences in Afghanistan to date attest that putting down insurgencies is not an easy matter for the USSR even with the advantages of relatively familiar terrain and fairly short supply lines.

A second use of Soviet forces might be against the white-minority government of South Africa. Were Moscow at the moment to try to mount a drive against South African forces on the territory that they now control, it could theoretically muster roughly 80 thousand men from all its airborne, air assault, and naval infantry units. To this total, one might add a potential 50 thousand troops from Cuba and another 10 thousand or so (one airborne division plus assorted other elements) from the GDR – the USSR's primary Communist allies in undertakings in sub-Saharan Africa.[162] Yet 140 thousand to 150 thousand troops would probably not suffice to defeat forces of the magnitude and sophistication that South Africa could mobilize. Only a commitment of substantial regular Soviet ground troops would reduce the risks to an acceptable level for Moscow. Providing adequate logistical backup for such a large military contingent, however, would be a considerable task at the distances entailed – even if the USSR managed to gain access to facilities in nearby states for transit purposes.

The third use of Soviet forces might be against the United States, acting in support of a black African country or South Africa. Here Moscow would face a difficult situation, for the United States enjoys some key advantages over the USSR in projecting its military power to remote theaters. For example, the United States can airlift twice as much, in terms of millions of ton-miles a day, as the Soviet Union, for U.S. transports have longer ranges than their Soviet counterparts and possess an in-flight refueling capability. The U.S. amphibious fleet boasts three times as much single-lift capacity as its Soviet counterpart. Not only is the U.S. Marine Corps 15 times as large as the Soviet Naval Infantry, but it can sustain operations for a month without resupply, as compared with a week for the Soviet forces. U.S. carrier-based aircraft greatly surpass the USSR's sea-based aircraft in range, endurance, and firepower. Finally, the capacity of the United States to conduct underway replenishment of aircraft while forces are in transit vastly exceeds that of the Soviet Union.[163]

The record of the last two decades, of course, suggests that Moscow will do its utmost to improve its power-projection capabilities in the years ahead. Such efforts are likely to be directed primarily toward technology. It appears inevitable, for example, that the 1980s will witness Soviet construction and deployment of a bigger and longer-range transport aircraft than exists in the USSR's present inventory. But there could be some expansion of human resources as well. Perhaps the most logical candidate for such treatment is the naval infantry forces. A total of just 12 thousand men scattered around four commands hardly seems appropriate for a state with global power pretensions.

Nonetheless, a combination of factors point to the likely persistence through the remainder of the decade of many current limitations on Moscow's capabilities to project power to sub-Saharan Africa. Like the United States, the USSR has evidently discovered that the increasing technological sophistication of weapons and equipment means higher per unit costs.[164] Thus, in the future it will probably have to settle for fewer new procurement programs and/or smaller production runs for items to be incorporated into the military inventory. This is especially true if, as most Western analysts anticipate, the growth rate of the Soviet economy fails to show a pronounced upward swing during the next few years. Yet present trends indicate that Soviet leaders may face a substantial military buildup in the West, and particularly the United States, during the rest of the 1980s. There could even be technological breakthroughs in connection with this buildup—notably in the domain of strategic defense—that would turn out to be disadvantageous to the USSR. Such considerations would place a premium, in Moscow's eyes, on procurement programs designed to maintain the existing central military balance. Under these circumstances, funding for attempts to beef up Soviet forces to project power over long distances could become much less available than it has been in the recent past.

6

The Outlook

Despite the foregoing constraints on their freedom of choice, Soviet leaders will still enjoy substantial leeway to decide what opportunities to pursue in sub-Saharan Africa, how actively to do so, and what means to employ. In trying to assess the likely nature of their decisions on these issues, however, it is important to bear in mind that these decisions will not take place in a vacuum. They will depend at least in part on considerations that have nothing to do with the merits of the situations per se. Such considerations include the timing of opportunities, the degree of Moscow's concern with internal matters, and the Soviet evaluation of the correlation of forces. Therefore, any meaningful estimate of how Soviet leaders will probably come down on issues regarding openings in sub-Saharan Africa must be set within the framework of these considerations.

Timing of Opportunities

The timing of opportunities can affect in a variety of ways Soviet calculations about how to approach them. If several major openings develop more or less simultaneously, the odds are that some will receive more attention in Moscow than others. Certainly, Soviet leaders will probably not seek to capitalize on each of them with as intense an interest or with as many resources as it would if they cropped up in sequence at fairly wide intervals. If a number of minor opportunities arise and the USSR commits a fair amount of resources to take advantage of them, it may find itself without sufficient resources to exploit a highly significant one that materializes later. Consequently, it may have either to renege on its prior commitments or to allow the new opportunity to pass unexploited. If two attractive openings appear at the same juncture but require conflicting courses of action to pursue, Moscow will in all likelihood perceive a need to select one or the other upon which to try to capitalize. Otherwise, it might compromise its ability to take advantage of either. These illustrations by no means exhaust the list.

Yet it is impossible to predict when any specific opportunity might emerge. Indeed, no one can say with certainty that it will even arise. One can only talk in terms of probabilities in this regard.

Thus, the impact of the timing factor on what Soviet leaders will opt to do with respect to sub-Saharan Africa in the rest of the 1980s remains unclear. About the most that one can offer in the nature of an appraisal is that the effect will be significant.

The Role of Domestic Affairs

Soviet leaders, like the leaders of all states, must strike a balance between the heed that they pay to internal matters and the attention that they devote to external events, and that balance shifts over time. Historically, domestic circumstances have provided the catalyst for the shifts.

Today, Soviet domestic conditions suggest that if any big changes take place in the balance of Moscow's concerns over the next few years, they will be in the direction of greater preoccupation with internal affairs. Moreover, just two issues at present appear potentially capable of bringing about such a development: the political succession and the state of the economy.

Although Yuri Andropov took over as general secretary of the CPSU after Leonid Brezhnev's death in November 1982, leadership transitions in the USSR, as countless commentators have observed, normally entail a fairly protracted power struggle, and many signs indicate that this one will probably conform to the rule. In terms of qualifications and experience, Andropov has weaknesses as the heir to Brezhnev's mantle, although he suffers no more disabilities in this regard than any other candidate. Furthermore, Brezhnev during the last months of his life appears to have promoted an old crony, Konstantin Chernenko, for the job, and Chernenko continues to occupy a prominent place within the highest political councils — evidently the second-ranking position in the hierarchy. Finally, Andropov, because of his long tenure as head of the Committee for State Security (KGB), lacks reliable proteges in other institutions, and particularly the party apparatus, who might afford him a solid base for consolidating his authority.[166]

Other factors could prolong the struggle even more than usual. At the time of his appointment to the general secretaryship, Andropov was already 68 years old, and he has not been in the best of health in recent years. If he were to die before he succeeded in consolidating his position, his replacement would in all likelihood face challenges from rivals and have to engage in a battle to firm up his own status. Such a battle could become an unusually long and difficult one. Although the age of the present top leadership affords Andropov the chance to fill many high-level posts with his own men in the near future, he might well exhaust this advantage before he passed from the political scene. Thus, a successor to Andropov could find his own room for maneuver severely curtailed.

The longer that a leadership transition goes on, of course, the greater the danger that it could produce a heated struggle. Such a struggle, in turn, could absorb a large share of the time and energies of the Kremlin, thereby reducing its attention to external affairs.

Mention has already been made of the declining growth rates of GNP and productivity in the USSR. These major economic problems are compounded by specific trends in the labor force. The working-age population has been expanding at an exceptionally low rate in recent years and promises to continue to do so well beyond the end of this decade; moreover, most additions to the labor force in the years immediately ahead will come from the non-Russian, especially Muslim, peoples of the USSR, who reside far from the country's industrial heartland.[166] Together, these difficulties point up the need for the transformation of the Soviet economy from an extensive-growth mechanism to an intensive-growth one.

The Soviet leadership could conceivably move to address this need in a concerted fashion at some juncture during the 1980s. If it did so, the magnitude of the undertaking would almost inevitably mean that there would be heightened emphasis on domestic matters at the expense of external concerns.

Several considerations, however, tend to mitigate the chances that Moscow will pay less heed to the outside world over the rest of the decade. In recent years, the USSR has made substantial progress toward upholding its claims to global power status, but that status is not yet firmly established. Under such circumstances, slackening the drive to achieve this goal would undoubtedly be psychologically difficult for Soviet leaders. Practical politics might well bolster their inhibitions. Over the last two decades, the Soviet military, whose prowess and accomplishments have been largely responsible for the USSR's strides toward global power status, has greatly increased its domestic political influence. Not only did at least some elements of the high command appear to have a role in the rise of Andropov to power, but some analysts now view the armed forces as the second most important institution in the Soviet political system, outranked only by the party apparatus.[167] Lastly, the economic troubles that the USSR has encountered to date have not convinced the Soviet leadership that it faces an economic crisis. This perception could change during the coming years, but there are probably enough things that the leadership can do at least to ameliorate the situation temporarily to avoid any reevaluations on this score for the remainder of the decade.[168]

The Correlation of Forces

In determining what course of action to pursue with regard to any opportunity that presents itself, Moscow must weigh the risks involved in each alternative open to the USSR. Fundamental to such calculations, from the Soviet standpoint, is an appraisal of the correlation of forces. This, in Soviet eyes, should encompass not only the local or regional situation but also the larger global context. Moreover, it requires a look at political, economic, and social conditions as well as straightforwardly military circumstances.

Today, Soviet officials display far less optimism about how sub-Saharan Africans will view Soviet behavior in the region than was the case just a few years ago. During the last half of the 1970s, the degree of local acceptance of Soviet activities in Angola in 1975–1976 and the Horn in 1977–1978 seems to have convinced Moscow that the USSR's claims to be the "natural ally" of the nonaligned world were meeting with growing favor among the black-ruled countries of sub-Saharan Africa,[169] and it tended to operate with mounting self-assurance and boldness in the area. But the vigor of the regional denunciation of the Soviet invasion of Afghanistan in December 1979 shook Moscow's confidence on this score. Robert Mugabe's coolness toward the USSR after his victory in the 1980 Zimbabwe elections also had a sobering impact in Moscow. Thus, since 1980 Soviet officials have deemed a fairly high degree of circumspection desirable in their approach to black African states.

A similar decline in optimism about the Western, and especially the U.S., reaction to Soviet undertakings in the area has resulted from the shift in the overall posture of the United States toward the USSR in the wake of the Soviet invasion of Afghanistan. During the Angolan civil war of 1975–1976 and the crisis in 1977–1978 over Somalia's invasion of the Ogaden, the United States had eschewed a military commitment to prevent Soviet-backed Cuban forces from resolving the conflicts to the benefit of Soviet clients. However, Afghanistan triggered a change in the U.S. mood. Not only did Washington take diplomatic and economic reprisals against Moscow—for example, a boycott of the 1980 Olympic games and an embargo on grain shipments to the USSR—but it also warned Soviet officials that it would resist any Soviet effort to move into the Persian Gulf. To bolster that declaration, it instituted a buildup of U.S. military forces. That buildup has been accelerated and expanded since the Reagan administration assumed office. Such a trend of events has reinforced Moscow's inclination to behave discreetly in sub-Saharan Africa.

These Soviet perceptions, to be sure, might alter in the future, but they will probably not do so unless the current attitudes of most black African rulers and/or the United States shift. Just what the longevity of these attitudes will be is impossible to say, for a host of factors could lead to changes in them. Perhaps the most prominent illustration at the moment is the U.S.-South African relationship. If the United States becomes so identified with South Africa in the minds of the leaders of the black African countries, then many of these leaders who are skeptical of the USSR as a "natural ally" could revise their thinking on the issue. Nevertheless, a lot of other factors could be cited as well.

Conclusion

Insofar as one can discern, then, there will be no compelling reason for the USSR to refrain from efforts to exploit opportunities that crop up in sub-Saharan Africa during the rest of the 1980s. On the contrary, the continuing Soviet drive for great power status will give Moscow a major incentive to take whatever advantage it can of these openings.

Yet it would also appear that Soviet leaders will probably tend to be discriminating in approaching these opportunities. This is true not only with respect to which of these they will actually pursue but also with regard to how intensely and by what means they will do so. In particular, it seems likely that the USSR will behave somewhat more cautiously, or at least less boldly, than it did during the late 1970s.

If this general assessment is correct, the chances of some growth of Soviet involvement in the region are good. The USSR, it is true, could suffer some reverses in the area in the years ahead, but in view of the lengthy list of opportunities that could arise, it seems unlikely that the reverses will offset the gains that Moscow will register from the new openings.

At the same time, any expansion of the Soviet role in the region will probably be of a moderate sort. Only in Southern Africa do there appear to be potential opportunities that rival those of which the USSR availed itself in the late 1970s.

Notes

1. U.S. Central Intelligence Agency (CIA), *Communist Aid Activities in Non-Communist Less Developed Countries, 1979 and 1954–79*, ER 80–10318U (Washington, D.C., October 1980), p. 39.

2. Calculated by the author from information in *The International Transfer of Conventional Arms*, A Report to the Congress from the U.S. Arms Control and Disarmament Agency (ACDA) (Washington, D.C.: GPO, 1974), pp. A-5, A-13, and A-14.

3. CIA, *Communist Aid Activities in Non-Communist Less Developed Countries, 1979 and 1954–79*, p. 10.

4. Ibid., p. 6.

5. Ibid., p. 11.

6. Ibid., p. 24.

7. See data in ACDA, *The International Transfer of Conventional Arms*, pp. A-5 and A-13.

8. The USSR expanded this list further in the 1980s with the opening of formal links with Lesotho in 1980 and Zimbabwe in 1981.

9. In 1981, the USSR entered into a similar treaty with the People's Republic of the Congo, raising the number of operational instruments once again to four.

10. Drawn from various Soviet and African press reports.

11. For Soviet discussion of these ties, see, for example, K.N. Brutents, *Osvobodivshiesia strany v 70-e gody* (Moscow: Izdatel'stvo politicheskoi literatury, 1979), pp. 142–143; C. P. Nemanov, "Partii avangardnogo tipa v Afrikanskikh stranakh sotsialisticheskoi orientatsii," *Narody Azii i Afriki*, no. 2 (1979): 27; B. Ponomarev, "Sovmestnaia bor'ba rabochego i natsional'no-osvoboditel'nogo dvizhenii imperializma, za social'nyi progress," *Kommunist*, no. 16 (November 1980):42–43.

12. CIA, *Communist Aid Activities in Non-Communist Less Developed Countries, 1979 and 1954–79*, p. 39.

13. Ibid., p. 10.

14. Ibid., p. 11.

15. Ibid., p. 24.

16. The former total was arrived at by the author on the basis of data in ACDA, *World Military Expenditures and Arms Transfers, 1970–1979* (Washington, D.C., March 1982), p. 127; the latter, on the basis of information in ACDA, *The International Transfer of Conventional Arms*, pp. A-13, and A-14.

17. The statistics in the preceding paragraph were derived by the author from data in ACDA, *The International Transfer of Conventional Arms*, pp. A-13 and A-14; ACDA, *World Military Expenditures and Arms Transfers, 1970–1979*, p. 127.

18. This discussion relies on information in ACDA, *World Military Expenditures and Arms Transfers, 1970–1979*, p. 127, and, in the case of the liberation movements, on a wide number of reports in the Western press.

19. CIA, *Communist Aid Activities in Non-Communist Less Developed Countries, 1979 and 1954–79*, p. 6.

20. Calculated by the author on the basis of data in ibid., p. 16, and CIA, *Communist Aid to Less Developed Countries of the Free World, 1977*, ER 78-10478U (Washington, D.C., November 1978), p. 4.

21. See, for instance, James M. McConnell and Bradford Dismukes, "Soviet Diplomacy of Force in the Third World," *Problems of Communism* 28, no. 1 (January-February 1979):18; International Institute for Strategic Studies (IISS), *The Military Balance 1982–1983* (London: IISS, 1982), p. 16.

22. McConnell and Dismukes, "Soviet Diplomacy," p. 18.

23. For more extensive analysis of the Soviet-Cuban relationship, see David E. Albright, "The USSR, Its Communist Allies, and Southern Africa," *Munger Africana Library Notes,* no. 55 (November 1980):4–6; David E. Albright, "The Communist States and Southern Africa," in Gwendolen M. Carter and Patrick O'Meara, eds., *International Politics in Southern Africa* (Bloomington, Ind.: Indiana University Press, 1982), pp. 12–15; William J. Durch, *The Cuban Military in Africa and the Middle East: From Algeria to Angola,* Professional Paper No. 201 (Arlington, Va.: Center for Naval Analyses, September 1977); William M. LeoGrande, *Cuba's Policy in Africa, 1959–1980* (Berkeley: University of California Press, 1980); Edward Gonzalez, "Cuba, the Soviet Union, and Africa," in David E. Albright, ed., *Communism in Africa* (Bloomington, Ind.: Indiana University Press, 1980), pp. 145–167.

24. CIA, *Communist Aid Activities in Non-Communist Less Developed Countries, 1979 and 1954–79,* p. 15.

25. The ensuing discussion draws upon W. Scott Thompson, *Ghana's Foreign Policy 1957–1966* (Princeton, N.J.: Princeton University Press, 1969), especially pp. 162–413; Robert Legvold, *Soviet Policy in West Africa* (Cambridge, Mass.: Harvard University Press, 1970), particularly pp. 68–274; David E. Albright, *The Dilemmas of Courtship: The Soviet Union, China, and Ghana* (Indiana University Press, forthcoming), chs. 4 and 6; Ghana, *Nkrumah's Subversion in Africa* (Accra: Ministry of Information, 1966); Ghana, *Nkrumah's Deception of Africa* (Accra: Ministry of Information, 1967). Except where noted, precise documentation for specific details of the analysis may be found in these sources.

26. See Central Bureau of Statistics, *Annual Report on External Trade in Ghana* for the relevant years.

27. See ACDA, *The International Transfer of Conventional Arms,* p. A-13.

28. For further discussion, see Jiri Valenta, "Soviet Decision-Making on the Intervention in Angola," in Albright, *Communism in Africa,* especially pp. 112–116; CIA, *Communist Aid Activities in Non-Communist Less Developed Countries 1978,* ER 79-10412U (Washington, D.C., September 1979), pp. 21–22; CIA, *Communist Aid Activities in Non-Communist Less Developed Countries 1979 and 1954–79,* p. 39.

29. See, for example, *Newsweek*, March 20, 1978; David E. Albright, "The Horn of Africa and the Arab-Israeli Conflict," in Robert O. Freedman, ed., *World Politics and the Arab-Israeli Conflict* (Elmsford, N.Y.: Pergamon Press, 1979), pp. 166–170; Leo-Grande, *Cuba's Policy in Africa, 1959–1980*, pp. 37–45; Morris Rothenberg, *The USSR and Africa: New Dimensions of Soviet Global Power* (Washington, D.C.: Advanced International Studies Institute, 1980), pp. 137–147; CIA, *Communist Aid Activities in Non-Communist Less Developed Countries, 1979 and 1954–79*, pp. 15 and 40.

30. See Brutents, *Osvobodivshiesia strany v 70-e gody*, pp. 142–143; Nemanov, "Partii avangardnogo tipa v Afrikanskikh stranakh sotsialisticheskoi orientatsii," p. 27; B. Ponomarev, "Sovmestnaia bor'ba rabochego i natsional'no-osvoboditel'nogo dvizhenii imperializma, za social'nyi progress," pp. 42–43; Rothenberg, *The USSR and Africa*, ch. 7; William F. Robinson, "Eastern Europe's Presence in Black Africa," *Radio Free Europe Research*, Background Report no. 142 (June 21, 1979):4.

31. See Melvin Croan, "East Germany and Africa," in David E. Albright and Jiri Valenta, eds., *The Communist States and Africa* (Bloomington, Ind.: Indiana University Press, forthcoming).

32. See David E. Albright, "Moscow's African Policy of the 1970's," in Albright, *Communism in Africa*, pp. 50–51; IISS, *Strategic Survey 1980–1981* (London: IISS, 1981), p. 21.

33. CIA, *Communist Aid Activities in Non-Communist Less Developed Countries, 1979 and 1954–79*, pp. 18 and 39; David and Marina Ottaway, *Afrocommunism* (New York: Africana Publishing Company, 1981), pp. 175–176; *Washington Post*, December 31, 1981.

34. See International Monetary Fund (IMF), *Direction of Trade Statistics Yearbook 1981* (Washington, D.C.: IMF, 1981); the annual volumes of USSR Ministry of Foreign Trade, *Vneshniaia torgovlia SSSR* for 1975–1979 (Moscow: Statistika, 1976–1980); David and Marina Ottaway, *Afrocommunism*, ch. 7, passim. It is worth recording, however, that by 1982 Soviet sources were claiming that the socialist countries together accounted for 22 percent of Ethiopia's total trade turnover. See G. Galperin and V. Platov, "Revolutionary Transformation in Ethiopia," *International Affairs*, no. 6 (June 1982):65.

35. See particularly Marina Ottaway, "The Theory and Practice of Marxism-Leninism in Mozambique and Ethiopia," in Albright, *Communism in Africa*, pp. 118–144; David and Marina Ottaway, *Afrocommunism*, chs. 4–7; Jay Ross in *Washington Post*, December 29, 1981.

36. See the sources cited in footnote 30.

37. For more extended treatment, with sources, of Mengistu's reluctance to form a vanguard party, see Albright, "Moscow's African Policy of the 1970's," pp. 60–61; Paul B. Henze, "Communism and Ethiopia," *Problems of Communism* 30, no. 3 (May-June 1981): 63–64; Rothenberg, *The USSR and Africa*, pp. 147–152.

38. See, for instance, David and Marina Ottaway, *Afrocommunism*, p. 175; Jay Ross in *Washington Post*, December 31, 1981.

39. CIA, *Communist Aid Activities in Non-Communist Less Developed Countries, 1979 and 1954–79*, p. 21.

40. ACDA, *World Military Expenditures and Arms Transfers 1970–1979*, p. 127.

41. CIA, *Communist Aid Activities in Non-Communist Less Developed Countries, 1979 and 1954–79*, pp. 15 and 39.

42. Calculated by the author from data in CIA, *Communist Aid to the Less Developed Countries of the Free World, 1977*, p. 4; CIA, *Communist Aid Activities in Non-Communist Less Developed Countries, 1979 and 1954–79*, p. 16.

43. CIA, *Communist Aid Activities in Non-Communist Less Developed Countries, 1979 and 1954–79*, p. 6.

44. See Colin Legum, "National Liberation in Southern Africa," *Problems of Communism* 24, no. 1 (January-February 1975):1–20; Colin Legum, "The Soviet Union, China and the West in Southern Africa," *Foreign Affairs* 54, no. 4 (July 1976):745–762; John A. Marcum, *The Angolan Revolution*, vol. 1 (Cambridge, Mass.: MIT Press, 1969) and Vol. 2 (Cambridge, Mass.: MIT Press, 1978).

45. See particularly Legum, "The Soviet Union, China and the West in Southern Africa," and Colin Legum, "The African Crisis," *Foreign Affairs* 57, no. 3 (America and the World 1978):640–641.

46. On the GDR's assumption of the function of primary arms supplier for ZAPU, see *Newsweek*, July 9, 1979.

47. See Valenta, "Soviet Decision-Making on the Intervention in Angola," pp. 112–116; Edward Gonzalez, "Cuban Policy Toward Africa: Activities, Motivations, and Outcomes," in Albright and Valenta, *The Communist States and Africa.*

48. For more detailed analysis, with sources, of the developments covered in the ensuing discussion, see Albright, "The Horn of Africa and the Arab-Israeli Conflict," especially pp. 158–168.

49. Interview of January 5, 1979 with David and Marina Ottaway, cited in David and Marina Ottaway, *Afrocommunism*, p. 9.

50. For more extended treatment of the shifts involved, see Colin Legum, "African Outlooks toward the USSR," in Albright, *Communism in Africa*, pp. 7–34.

51. See Colin Legum, ed., *Africa Contemporary Record 1975–76* (New York: Africana Publishing Co., 1976), p. B/365.

52. See Radio Luanda Domestic Service in Portuguese, December 9 and 10, 1978, in Foreign Broadcast Information Service (FBIS), *Daily Report: Sub-Saharan Africa* (hereafter *FBIS-SSA*), December 11, 1978, pp. A/1–2; Radio Luanda Domestic Service in Portuguese, December 10, 1978, in *FBIS-SSA*, December 12, 1978, pp. E/1–2; the Reuter dispatch and David Ottaway in *Washington Post*, December 10 and 15, 1978, respectively.

53. For discussion of this pressure and Mengistu's response, see Henze, "Communism and Ethiopia," pp. 63–64; Rothenberg, *The USSR and Africa*, pp. 147–152. Good examples of Mengistu's public commentary on the question may be found in his speech at a dinner in Moscow on November 17, 1978, and his address at a rally in Addis Ababa on May Day 1979, as reported, respectively, in *Pravda*, November 18, 1978, and by Radio Addis Ababa Domestic Service in Amharic, May 1, 1979, in *FBIS-SSA*, May 2, 1979, pp. B/1–2.

54. See Colin Legum, "Africa's Contending Revolutionaries," *Problems of Communism* 21, no. 2 (March-April 1972): 12–15.

55. On Soviet aid commitments, see CIA, *Communist Aid Activities in Non-Communist Less Developed Countries, 1979 and 1954–79*, p. 39, and George T. Yu, "Sino-Soviet Rivalry in Africa," in Albright, *Communism in Africa*, especially pp. 170–172. The

financial flows to the area from the Western industrial countries, the member states of OPEC, and multilateral agencies were calculated by the author on the basis of data in United Nations Conference on Trade and Development (UNCTAD), *Handbook of International Trade and Statistics, 1981 Supplement* (New York: United Nations, 1982).

56. Relevant country breakdowns of Soviet extensions of credits to sub-Saharan Africa may be found in CIA, *Communist Aid Activities in Non-Communist Less Developed Countries, 1979 and 1954-79*, p. 39. The financial flows to the region from the Western industrial countries, the member states of OPEC, and multilateral agencies were derived by the author from information in UNCTAD, *Handbook of International Trade and Statistics, 1981 Supplement.*

57. See the sources cited in footnote 38.

58. On the size of the Soviet, East European, and Cuban contingents of economic technicians in sub-Saharan Africa in 1979, see CIA, *Communist Aid Activities in Non-Communist Less Developed Countries, 1979 and 1954-79*, pp. 10 and 21. For the estimate of the British and French ones, see Guy Arnold, *Aid in Africa* (London and New York: Kogan Page/Nichols Publishing Co., 1979), p. 213.

59. CIA, *Communist Aid Activities in Non-Communist Less Developed Countries, 1979 and 1954-79*, p. 21.

60. For relevant discussion, see David and Marina Ottaway, *Afrocommunism*, pp. 168-176, and especially pp. 168-170.

61. All percentages calculated by the author from data in IMF, *Direction of Trade Statistics Yearbook 1981.*

62. For information on the leading trade partners of the USSR in sub-Saharan Africa, see the annual volumes of USSR Ministry of Foreign Trade, *Vneshniaia torgovlia SSR* for 1975-1979. Soviet shares of the trade of these countries were arrived at by the author on the basis of data in IMF, *Direction of Trade Statistics Yearbook 1981.*

63. Compiled from information in ACDA, *World Military Expenditures and Arms Transfers 1970-1979*, p. 127.

64. Ibid.

65. See Legum, *Africa Contemporary Record 1975–76*, p. B/365.

66. For more extended discussion, with sources, see Albright, "The Horn of Africa and the Arab-Israeli Conflict," pp. 162–166.

67. See ibid., pp. 168–170.

68. Soviet media hinted repeatedly, for instance, that efforts of this sort could generate pressure on the "national liberation" movements of the two countries to accede to conditions restricting their freedom of maneuver once they gained power.

69. For further details, see David E. Albright, "The USSR and Africa 1981: Disinclination to Assume New Responsibilities," in Colin Legum, ed., *Africa Contemporary Record, 1981–82* (London: Holmes and Meier, 1982); David E. Albright, "The USSR and Africa in 1982: Quest for Global Power Status," in Colin Legum, ed., *Africa Contemporary Record, 1982–83* (London: Holmes and Meier, forthcoming in 1983); *New York Times*, December 9, 1982.

70. On the agreements, see *Pravda*, May 21, 1981; *Sel'skaya zhizn'*, May 26, 1981; *Pravda*, January 21 and 25, 1982, For discussion of the projects planned to date under the terms of these agreements, see Albright, "The USSR and Africa in 1981"; Albright, "The USSR and Africa in 1982."

71. U.S. Department of State, Bureau of Intelligence and Research, *Soviet and East European Aid to the Third World, 1981* (Washington, D.C., February 1983), pp. 3, 12–13.

72. Radio Maputo Domestic Service in Portuguese, February 22, 1981, in FBIS, *Daily Report: Soviet Union* (hereafter *FBIS-SOV*), February 25, 1981, p. J/2; *New York Times*, December 10, 1981.

73. For elaboration, see Vernon V. Aspaturian, "Soviet Global Power and the Correlation of Forces," *Problems of Communism* 29, no. 3 (May–June 1980):1–18.

74. For background analysis, see Albright, "Moscow's African Policy of the 1970s," pp. 37–49. For a representative sampling of relevant Soviet commentary of the 1980s, see N. Gavrilov, "The New Africa Emerging," *International Affairs*, no. 7 (July 1980):32–39; Yu. N. Gavrilov, "Problemy formirovaniia avangardnoi partii v stranakh sotsialisticheskoi orientatsii," *Narody Azii*

i Afriki, no. 6 (1980):10–23; V1. Li, "Sotsial'nye revoliutsii v Afro-Aziatskikh stranakh i nauchnyi sotsializm," *Aziia i Afrika segodnia,* no. 3 (March 1981):2–5; G. Kim, "The National Liberation Movement Today," *International Affairs,* no. 4 (April 1981):27–37; Ye. Primakov, "Strany sotsialisticheskoi orientatsii: trudnyi, no real'nyi perekhod k sotsializmu," *Mirovaia ekonomika i mezhdunarodnye otnosheniia,* no. 7 (July 1981):3–16; Ye. Mel'nikov, "Politicheskie preobrazovaniia v Afrikanskikh stranakh sotsialisticheskoi orientatsii," ibid., no. 12 (December 1981):121–126.

75. For typical illustrations from the 1980s, see Gavrilov, "The New Africa Emerging," and Anat. Gromyko, "The Imperialist Threat to Africa," *International Affairs,* no. 7 (July 1981):47–53.

76. *Pravda,* April 4, 1971.

77. For an explicit statement of this view with regard to Africa as a whole, see M. L. Vishvevskii, "Politika Vashingtona v Afrike i Amerikansko-Afrikanskie izucheniia," *SShA,* January 1980, p. 118.

78. Soviet memorandum submitted to the UN by USSR Foreign Minister Gromyko on October 4, 1976, in *Pravda,* October 5, 1976.

79. For a good, detailed discussion of recent Soviet writings on Third World development, see Elizabeth Kridl Valkenier, "Development Issues in Recent Soviet Scholarship," *World Politics* 32, no. 4 (July 1980):485–508.

80. For a representative summary of the Soviet view, see T. Deich, "Afrika i Pekin," *Aziia i Afrika segodnia,* no. 12 (December 1981):16–19.

81. The distinction between interests and objectives here is crucial. A nation's objectives flow from its discerned interests, but the two are not necessarily identical. Some interests that a nation pinpoints may never become operational goals for diverse reasons. For instance, the nation may recognize that it lacks the capabilities to fulfill these interests, or the interests may be at odds with other interests that the nation regards as more important.

82. For more extended analysis of this period of Soviet policy, see Albright, "Moscow's African Policy of the 1970's," pp. 37–42; Albright, *The Dilemmas of Courtship,* chaps. 2, 4, and 6; Legvold, *Soviet Policy in West Africa,* pp. 40–330.

83. See Philip Crowson, *Non-Fuel Minerals and Foreign Policy* (London: Royal Institute of International Affairs, 1977); W.C.J. van Rensburg and D.A. Pretorius, *South Africa's Strategic Minerals – Pieces on a Continental Chessboard* (Johannesburg: Valiant Publishers, 1977); W.C.J. van Rensburg, "Africa and Western Lifelines," *Strategic Review*, Spring 1978; Congressional Research Service, U.S. Library of Congress, prepared for the U.S. Senate Foreign Relations Committee, Subcommittee on Africa, *Imports of Minerals from South Africa by the United States and the OECD Countries* (Washington, D.C.: GPO, 1980).

84. For typical illustrations, see V. Baryshnikov, "Raw Material Resources of Africa," *International Affairs*, no. 12 (December 1974); Dimitri Volsky, "Southern Version of NATO," *New Times*, no. 36 (September 1976); *Pravda*, January 18, 1982.

85. For more detailed discussions, with supporting data, see Jan Vanous, "East European Economic Slowdown," *Problems of Communism* 31, no. 4 (July-August 1982):1–19; U.S. Congress, Joint Economic Committee, *Soviet Economy in a Time of Change* (Washington, D.C.: GPO, 1979), vols. 1 and 2, especially the articles by Leslie Dienes, Marshall I. Goldman, J. Richard Lee and James R. Lecky, Michael R. Dohan, and Lawrence H. Theriot and JeNelle Matheson.

86. See the sources cited in footnote 83 plus Robert M. Price, "U.S. Policy toward Southern Africa: Interests, Choices, and Constraints," in Carter and O'Meara, *International Politics in Southern Africa*, particularly pp. 59–62.

87. See, for example, *Africa News*, October 13, 1980, pp. 6–7.

88. For illustrative purposes, see Baryshnikov, "Raw Material Resources of Africa"; Volsky, "Southern Version of NATO"; Anatoly Gromyko, "Africa in the Strategy of Neo-Colonialism," *International Affairs*, no. 11 (November 1978):84; V. Kudriavtsev in *Izvestiia*, May 4, 1979; Leonid Brezhnev's report to the twenty-sixth CPSU congress in February 1981, as carried in *Pravda*, February 24, 1981.

89. See, for instance, Brutents, *Osvobodivshiesia strany v 70-e gody*, pp. 67–77. Brutents has served as a deputy director of the International Department of the CPSU since the mid-1970s.

90. For elaboration and documentation, see David E. Albright, "Vanguard Parties in the Third World and Soviet Foreign Policy," in Walter Laqueur and Barry Rubin, eds., *The Pattern of Soviet Conduct in the Third World,* (New York: Praeger, forthcoming in 1983).

91. On East Germany, see Albright, "The Communist States and Southern Africa," pp. 4–15; Croan, "East Germany and Africa."

92. For more extended discussion, see Price, "U.S. Policy toward Southern Africa," pp. 59–67.

93. For a representative Soviet statement, see O. Bogomolov, "CMEA and the Developing World," *International Affairs,* no. 7 (July 1979):26–28.

94. See Albright, "Moscow's African Policy of the 1970's," pp. 50–51; Albright, "The USSR and Africa in 1981," passim; Albright, "The USSR and Africa in 1982," passim; IISS, *Strategic Survey 1980 1981,* p. 21.

95. For relevant treatment of Soviet force projection capabilities see Worth H. Bagley, "Sea Power and Western Security: The Next Decade," *Adelphi Papers,* no. 139 (1977):1–40; McConnell and Dismukes, "Soviet Diplomacy"; IISS, *Strategic Survey 1978* (London: IISS, 1979); IISS, *Strategic Survey 1980–1981* and *The Military Balance, 1982–1983.*

96. See, for example, Thompson, *Ghana's Foreign Policy, 1957–1966;* Ghana, *Nkrumah's Subversion in Africa;* Ghana, *Nkrumah's Deception of Africa.*

97. The World Bank, *Accelerated Development in Sub-Saharan Africa: An Agenda for Action* (Washington, D.C.: World Bank, 1981), p. 3.

98. See Arthur S. Banks et al., eds. *Economic Handbook of the World: 1981* (New York: McGraw-Hill, 1981); George Thomas Kurian, *Encyclopedia of the Third World* (New York: Facts on File, 1978).

99. Directorate of Intelligence, CIA, *Handbook of Economic Statistics, 1982,* CPAS 82–10006 (Washington, D.C., September 1982), p. 2.

100. Drawn from *Encyclopedia of the Third World* and *Economic Handbook of the World, 1981.*

101. UNCTAD, *Handbook of International Trade and Development Statistics, Supplement 1981*, pp. 354–359.

102. The data in this paragraph are drawn from World Bank, *Accelerated Development in Sub-Saharan Africa*, pp. 48, 166, and 176.

103. For more detailed treatment of these issues, see ibid., chaps. 4 and 7.

104. See ibid., pp. 17–21 and 159.

105. Ibid., pp. 17–18 and 159.

106. Sean M. Cleary, "Third World Development: A Cautious Prognosis," *Vital Speeches* 49, no. 10 (March 1, 1983):294.

107. See, for instance, Gwendolen M. Carter, *Which Way Is South Africa Going?* (Bloomington, Ind.: Indiana University Press, 1980); Colin Legum, "The End of Apartheid," *The Washington Quarterly* (Winter 1982): 169–178. Both of these writers, it should be underscored, have long records as critics of apartheid in South Africa.

108. Compiled from ACDA, *World Military Expenditures and Arms Transfers 1970-1979*, pp. 48–84; ACDA, *World Military Expenditures and Arms Trade 1963-1973* (Washington, D.C.: GPO, 1975), pp. 20–66.

109. Calculated from data in ACDA, *World Military Expenditures and Arms Transfers 1970-1979*, p. 127, and ACDA, *The International Transfer of Conventional Arms*, p. A-7.

110. For more detailed treatment of the evolution of Soviet thinking about opportunities in the Third World, see Albright, "Moscow's African Policy in the 1970s"; Albright, "The Middle East and Africa in Recent Soviet Policy," in Roger E. Kanet, ed., *Soviet Foreign Policy in the 1980s* (New York: Praeger, 1982), pp. 295–300; and Albright, "The Soviet Role in Africa from Moscow's Perspective," in Albright and Valenta, *The Communist States and Africa.*

111. For analysis of the evolution of the Soviet role in the Horn, see Albright, "The Horn of Africa and the Arab-Israeli Conflict"; Rothenberg, *The USSR and Africa*, pp. 33–50; Richard Remnek, "Soviet Policy in the Horn of Africa: The Decision to Intervene," in Robert H. Donaldson, ed., *The Soviet Union and the Third World: Success and Failure* (Boulder, Colo.: Westview, 1980), pp. 135–149.

112. The following discussion draws upon *Africa Confidential*, March 11, 1981; Henze, "Communism and Ethiopia," pp. 63–74; *Economist*, November 28, 1981, pp. 34 and 37; the reports of Jay Ross in *Washington Post*, December 31, 1981, and Pranay B. Gupte in *New York Times*, December 21, 1981; *Pravda*, January 2 and 8, 1983; Radio Moscow in English to Africa, January 8, 1983, in *FBIS-MEA*, January 10, 1983, p. J/1; *Economist Foreign Report*, January 20, 1983, p. 6; Department of State, *Soviet and East European Aid to the Third World, 1981*, p. 17.

113. Commentaries in the Soviet media during the first half of 1982 indicate that Moscow watched with interest the mounting instability in Somalia, and by the summer of that year Soviet authorities were expressing sympathy for the opposition Democratic Front for the Salvation of Somalia (DFSS). This identification with the opposition increased after late July, when Siad Barre turned to the United States for military assistance to counter an invading force composed largely of regular Ethiopian troops but including some DFSS elements. Soviet media repeatedly accused Siad Barre of bringing in the United States to crush a "national uprising" against his policies. See, for instance, the radio broadcasts carried in *FBIS-SOV* during 1982.

114. Data from UNCTAD, *Handbook of International Trade and Development Statistics, Supplement 1981*, p. 357; World Bank, *Accelerated Development in Sub-Saharan Africa*, p. 167; Anthony J. Hughes, "Reagan and Africa: Policy Options in the Horn," *Horn of Africa* 4, no. 2 (1981):5; the report of Alan Cowell in *New York Times*, September 25, 1981; The Economist Intelligence Unit, *Quarterly Economic Review of Uganda, Ethiopia, Somalia, Djibouti*, issues for 1980–1982.

115. See World Bank, *Accelerated Development in Sub-Saharan Africa*, p. 176; Cowell in *New York Times*, September 25, 1981.

116. For more detailed discussion of the refugee issue, see "Somalia: One in Three a Refugee," *Horn of Africa* 4, no. 1 (1981): 46–51; Cowell in *New York Times*, September 25, 1981; W.A.E. Skurnik, "Continuing Problems in Africa's Horn," *Current History* 82, no. 482 (March 1983):121.

117. On these various sources of discontent with the Mogadishu government, see, for example, *Africa Confidential*, March 11, 1981, and September 8, 1982; Hughes, "Reagan and Africa"; *Defense and Foreign Affairs Daily*, February 22, 1982; the program of the DFSS adopted at its first congress, February 28-March 1, 1983, as broadcast by the clandestine Radio Halgan in Somali to Somalia, March 8, 1983, and reported in *FBIS-MEA*, March 15, 1983, pp. R/3-9. The figures on U.S. military aid to Somalia come from the Department of Defense's presentation to Congress on *Security Assistance Programs, FY 1984*, p. 287.

118. For these developments, see, for instance, *Africa Confidential*, March 11, 1981, and September 8, 1982; Hughes, "Reagan and Africa"; *FBIS-MEA*, October 20, 1981, pp. R/2-4, and October 21, 1981, pp. R/1-6; *Washington Post*, February 12, 1982; *Defense and Foreign Affairs Daily*, February 22, 1982; Gerald Funk, "Some Observations on Strategic Realities and Ideological Red Herrings on the Horn of Africa," *CSIS Africa Notes*, no. 1 (Washington, D.C.: Center for Strategic and International Studies [CSIS], July 1, 1982); *New York Times*, October 8, 1982; *Africa Report*, March-April 1983, p. 29; Skurnik, "Continuing Problems in Africa's Horn," pp. 121-122.

119. *Africa Confidential*, March 11, 1981. For discussion of the continuing turmoil within the Front, see ibid., September 8, 1982.

120. *Washington Post*, February 12, 1982; *Defense and Foreign Affairs Daily*, February 22, 1982; *Africa Confidential*, September 8, 1982; *New York Times*, October 8, 1982; Skurnik, "Continuing Problems in Africa's Horn," pp. 121-122.

121. See, for example, *Africa Confidential*, March 11, 1981; *FBIS-MEA*, March 3, 1982; Skurnik, "Continuing Problems in Africa's Horn," pp. 121-122.

122. See *FBIS-MEA*, March 15, 1983, pp. R/3-9.

123. Concerning Soviet involvement in Zaire since 1960, see, for instance, Catherine Hoskyns, *The Congo Since Independence, January 1960-December 1961* (London: Oxford University Press, 1965); Thompson, *Ghana's Foreign Policy, 1957-1966*, pp. 119-161; Crawford Young, *Politics in the Congo: Decolonization and Inde-*

pendence (Princeton, N.J.: Princeton University Press, 1965); Young, "Zaire: the Unending Crisis," *Foreign Affairs* 57, no. 1 (Fall 1978): 167–185; Howard M. Epstein, ed., *Revolt in the Congo, 1960–64* (New York: Facts on File, 1965).

124. Young, "Zaire: the Unending Crisis," p. 179.

125. Ibid., p. 176; "Report on Situation of the Zaire Armed Forces Submitted by Former Prime Minister Nguza," in *Political and Economic Situation in Zaire – Fall 1981: Hearing before the Subcommittee on Africa of the Committee on Foreign Affairs, House of Representatives, 97th Cong., 1st sess., September 15, 1981* (Washington, D.C.: G.P.O., 1982), pp. 44–46; *Washington Post,* November 8, 1981.

126. UNCTAD, *Handbook of International Trade and Development Statistics, Supplement 1981,* p. 356; CIA, *Handbook of Economic Statistics,* 1982, p. 2; World Bank, *Accelerated Development in Sub-Saharan Africa,* pp. 166–167; Young, "Zaire: the Unending Crisis," pp. 171–177; Committee on Foreign Affairs, *Political and Economic Situation in Zaire – Fall 1981,* pp. 5–6, 31–36; the reports of Don Oberdorfer and Leon Dash in *Washington Post,* September 15 and November 8 and 11, 1981; *Zaire: A Staff Report to the Committee on Foreign Relations, United States Senate, July 1982* (Washington, D.C.: GPO, 1982), pp. 1–2.

127. World Bank, *Accelerated Development in Sub-Saharan Africa,* p. 176.

128. Young, "Zaire: the Unending Crisis," pp. 171–172; Carey Winfrey in *New York Times,* November 13, 1979; *Zaire: A Staff Report to the Committee on Foreign Relations,* pp. 7–9.

129. Winfrey in *New York Times,* November 13, 1979; *Wall Street Journal,* June 3, 1980; "Zaire," *Foreign Economic Trends and Their Implications for the United States,* August 1980; *Zaire: A Staff Report to the Committee on Foreign Relations,* pp. 8–9; *Africa Report,* March-April 1983, p. 31.

130. "Zaire"; *Zaire: A Staff Report to the Committee on Foreign Relations,* p. 9; Radio Kinshasa AZAP in French, December 8, 1982, in *FBIS-MEA,* December 9, 1982, pp. S/1–5.

131. See, for example, Young, "Zaire: the Unending Crisis," pp. 172–174; *Political and Economic Situation in Zaire – Fall 1981,* pp. 6, 37–39; Jay Ross in *Washington Post,* April 7, 1982; *Zaire:*

A Staff Report to the Committee on Foreign Relations, pp. 1–2, 7–8.

132. See, for instance, Chislain Kabwit, "The Growth of Internal and External Opposition to the Mobutu Regime," in Guy Gran, ed., *Zaire: The Political Economy of Underdevelopment* (New York: Praeger, 1979), pp. 290–291; Leon Dash and Jay Ross in *Washington Post,* November 8, 1981, and April 7, 1982, respectively; Committee on Foreign Affairs, *Political and Economic Situation in Zaire,* passim.

133. Young, "Zaire: the Unending Crisis," pp. 170–174, 178–179; Committee on Foreign Affairs, *Political and Economic Situation in Zaire,* p. 8; *Washington Post,* November 8, 1981; *Zaire: A Staff Report to the Committee on Foreign Relations,* pp. 1–4.

134. See Leon Dash and Don Oberdorfer, *Washington Post,* November 8 and December 1, 1981, respectively; Paris Agence France Presse (AFP) in English, January 19, 1983, and Paris AFP in French, January 23, 1983, in *FBIS-MEA,* January 20, 1983, pp. S/2–3, and January 24, 1983, pp. S/1–2, respectively.

135. For discussion of the available evidence on this score, see, for instance, Young, "Zaire: the Unending Crisis," pp. 182–183.

136. For relevant data on the Soviet share of transfers of weapons and equipment to Southern Africa, see ACDA, *World Military Expenditures and Arms Transfers 1970–79* plus Western press reports such as *Newsweek,* July 9, 1979, and *Washington Post,* August 19, 1980.

137. *Facts on File* 41, no. 2106 (March 10, 1981):102.

138. On the ANC, see Study Commission on U.S. Policy Toward Southern Africa, *South Africa: Time Running Out* (Berkeley: University of California Press, 1981), p. 178; Legum, "'National Liberation' in Southern Africa," pp. 17–18. On Soviet contacts with Buthelezi, see Umtata Capital Radio in English, November 2, 1982, in *FBIS-MEA,* November 2, 1982, p. U/1.

139. Study Commission, *South Africa: Time Running Out,* pp. 128–129; Kenneth W. Grundy, "South Africa in the Political Economy of Southern Africa," in Carter and O'Meara, *International Politics of Southern Africa,* p. 148.

140. U.S. Department of State, Bureau of Intelligence and Research, *South Africa's Economic Involvement with Sub-Saharan*

Africa, Report no. 1257 (Washington, D.C., October 23, 1979); Study Commission, *South Africa: Time Running Out,* chap. 12; Grundy, "South Africa in the Political Economy of Southern Africa," pp. 167–176; Africa Institute of South Africa, *Southern Africa: Facts and Figures* (Pretoria, n.d.); Margaret A. Novicki, "Zimbabwe: The Economic Outlook," *Africa Report,* January-February 1983, p. 11; *Africa Report,* March-April 1983, pp. 36–37.

141. See IISS, *The Military Balance 1982*-1983; Chester A. Crocker, "Current and Projected Military Balances in Southern Africa," in Richard E. Bissell and Chester A. Crocker, eds., *South Africa into the 1980's* (Boulder, Colo.: Westview, 1979); W. Scott Thompson and Brett Silvers, "South Africa in Soviet Strategy," in ibid.

142. On SADCC, see Grundy, "South Africa in the Political Economy of Southern Africa," pp. 160–167; Philip L. Christenson, "Toward a Regional Economy," *African Index* 3, no. 22 (December 31, 1980); Bryan Silberman, "SADCC: A Status Report," *CSIS Africa Notes,* no. 11, April 5, 1983.

143. See IISS, *The Military Balance,* issues for 1980–1981 through 1982–1983.

144. For more detailed discussion, see particularly Albright, "Soviet Policy Toward Africa in 1981."

145. *Christian Science Monitor,* February 24, 1983.

146. For the growth rates for 1966–1970 through 1976–1980, see CIA, *Handbook of Economic Statistics, 1982,* pp. 68–69. The estimates for 1981–1982 come from Daniel L. Bond and Herbert S. Levine, "The Soviet Domestic Economy in the 1980s," a paper prepared for a conference on "The Soviet Economy and Military Spending" in Washington, D.C. under the auspices of the United States Information Agency, on February 4, 1983, to be published in a volume on the Soviet Union in the 1980s edited by Helmut Sonnenfeldt.

147. CIA, *Handbook of Economic Statistics, 1982,* p. 72.

148. For further discussion, see Bond and Levine, "The Soviet Domestic Economy in the 1980s."

149. CIA, *Handbook of Economic Statistics, 1982,* p. 26; Bond and Levine, "The Soviet Domestic Economy in the 1980s."

150. CIA, *Communist Aid Activities in Non-Communist Less Developed Countries, 1979 and 1954-79*, p. 7; Department of State, *Soviet and East European Aid to the Third World, 1981*, p. 17.

151. For data on the flow from non-Communist sources, see UNCTAD, *Handbook of International Trade and Statistics, 1981 Supplement*, pp. 290-297.

152. Data on Soviet imports by shares of commodity groups may be found in Vienna Institute for Comparative Economic Studies, ed., *Comecon Data 1981* (Westport, Conn.: Greenwood Press, 1982), p. 385. The annual averages for 1971-1975 are provided in the source; those for 1976-1979 and 1976-1980 were calculated by the author.

153. Ibid., p. 364.

154. Calculated by the author from data in USSR Ministry of Foreign Trade, *Vneshniaia torgovlia SSSR v 1979 g.*, p. 13.

155. For an articulate statement of both perspectives, see Bond and Levine, "The Soviet Domestic Economy in the 1980's."

156. For further discussion, see ibid.

157. CIA, *Communist Aid Activities in Non-Communist Less Developed Countries, 1979 and 1954-79*, p. 7; Department of State, *Soviet and East European Aid to the Third World, 1981*, p. 17. Soviet aid offerings to Third World countries averaged $1,624 million a year in 1975-1979, but the figure fell to $1,258 million a year in 1980-1981.

158. See, for example, the statement of Donald Burton, chief of the Military Economics Division of the CIA, in *Soviet Defense Expenditures and Related Programs, Hearings before the Subcommittee on General Procurement of the Committee on Armed Services, United States Senate, 96th Cong. 1st and 2nd sess., November 1, 8, 1979; February 4, 1980* (Washington, D.C.: GPO, 1980), pp. 40-43; Edward J. Laurence, "Soviet Arms Transfers to Sub-Saharan Africa: Patterns, Purposes, and Effects," in Albright and Valenta, *The Communist States and Africa*.

159. See, for instance, Bagley, "Sea Power and Western Security: The Next Decade"; James L. Moulton, "The Capability for Long-Range Intervention," in Michael MccGwire and John McDon-

nell, eds., *Soviet Naval Influence: Domestic and Foreign Dimensions* (New York: Praeger, 1977); Charles G. Pritchard, "Soviet Amphibious Force Projection," in ibid.; McConnell and Dismukes, "Soviet Diplomacy"; IISS, *Strategic Survey 1978, Strategic Survey 1980–1981,* and *The Military Balance, 1982–1983;* Coit D. Blacker, "Soviet Military Forces," in Robert Byrnes, ed., *After Brezhnev: Sources of Soviet Conduct in the 1980s* (Bloomington, Ind.: Indiana University Press, 1983).

160. For the numbers in this analysis, see IISS, *The Military Balance, 1982–1983;* Gonzalez, "Cuba, the Soviet Union, and Africa."

161. See "Third World Arms Production," *World Military Expenditures and Arms Transfers, 1969–1978* (Washington, D.C.: December 1980), pp. 19–21.

162. For the numbers in this discussion, see the sources cited in footnote 160.

163. IISS, *Strategic Survey 1978* and *Strategic Survey 1980–1981;* Blacker, "Soviet Military Forces"; Douglas Aircraft Company, *USAF/McDonnell Douglas C-17* (Long Beach, Calif.: McDonnell Douglas, n.d.).

164. See the statement of Donald Burton in Committee on Armed Services, *Soviet Defense Expenditures and Related Programs,* p. 45.

165. For relevant discussion and analysis, see the collection of articles on "The Andropov Succession" in *Problems of Communism* 32, no. 1 (January–February 1983):1–39.

166. See Abram Bergson, "Soviet Economic Slowdown and the 1981–85 Plan," *Problems of Communism* 30, no. 3 (May-June 1981):28–29; Murray Feshbach, "Between the Lines of the 1979 Soviet Census," *Problems of Communism* 31, no. 1 (January-February 1981):27–37.

167. See the symposium on "The Andropov Succession," in *Problems of Communism* 32, no. 1.

168. For more extended treatment of this issue, see Bond and Levine, "The Soviet Domestic Economy in the 1980's"; Joseph S. Berliner, "Managing the USSR Economy: Alternative Models," *Problems of Communism* 32, no. 1 (January-February 1983):40–56.

169. For more detailed treatment of Soviet efforts to persuade nonaligned states of this affinity, see William M. LeoGrande, "Evolution of the Nonaligned Movement," *Problems of Communism* 29, no. 1 (January-February 1980):35–52.